Companion Planting Secrets
Organic Gardening To Deter Pests And Increase Yields

Jason Johns

Visit me at www.GardeningWithJason.com for gardening tips and advice or follow me at www.YouTube.com/OwningAnAllotment for my video diary and tips. Join me on Facebook at www.Facebook.com/OwningAnAllotment.

Follow me on Instagram and Twitter as @allotmentowner for regular updates, tips and to ask your gardening questions.

If you have enjoyed this book, please leave a review on Amazon. I read each review personally and the feedback helps me to continually improve my books and provide you with more helpful books to read.

Once you have read this book, you will be offered a chance to download one of my books for free. Please turn to the back of the book to find out how to get your free book.

© 2020 Jason Johns

All rights reserved.

TABLE OF CONTENTS

Introduction 1
Companion Planting With Vegetables 11
Companion Planting With Flowers 35
Companion Planting With Herbs 48
Companion Planting With Trees 63
Companion Planting for Pest Control 66
Allelopathy Explained 72
Attracting Beneficial Insects 75
The Importance of Crop Rotation 89
Beneficial Weeds 93
Endnote 98
About Jason 101
Other Books By Jason 103
Want More Inspiring Gardening Ideas? 109
Free Book! 109

INTRODUCTION

Companion planting has been used by traditional farmers and home gardeners for centuries. In today's modern, scientific world, much of companion planting is ignored in favor of high yields and neat rows of plants smothered in chemicals for maximum yield with minimum effort. However, companion planting is very effective, helping to prevent pests and diseases while increasing yield and improving taste and all without a chemical in sight.

What is companion planting?

Firstly, it is not about giving your plants company to stop them from being lonely as they grow.

It's the technique of planting a different species of plant near to another in the knowledge that this benefits one or both plants. Effectively, it's about putting two plants near each other, so they help each other out in a number of different ways.

Although the history of companion planting is long, the scientific mechanisms behind it were not originally understood. In most cases, companion planting has been developed through testing, by 'secrets' passed down through a family and oral traditions. Despite the lack of scientific development, companion planting works, and many of the traditional companion plants are surprisingly effective when subjected to scientific investigation. Companion planting does help to reduce the incidence of pests and diseases as well as keeping the soil healthy.

As a gardener, you may have heard of the three sisters method of planting corn, beans, and pumpkins. This is an example of companion planting. The three plants grown together help each other. The sweet corn provides a pole for the beans to grow up; the beans trap nitrogen in the soil which benefits the pumpkins. The pumpkins cover the ground with their leaves which suppress weeds and helps to retain moisture.

You may also have heard about planting marigolds near to your tomatoes, or basil. Both of which provide benefit to the tomato plants in the form of protection improving the flavor.

There are lots of different types of companion planting. As you read this book, you will learn lots of different plants that work well together, many of which you probably already grow in your garden, just not together. Although they are not a miracle cure, they do provide some benefits and help to reduce the amount of chemicals needed for your plants.

Many of us garden away, completely unaware of companion planting. Sometimes, purely by accident, we'll plant two crops together that help each other, get a bumper crop and wonder what we did. Conversely, and I know I've done this, you plant two crops together and wonder why they do so badly, putting it down to poor weather, bad seeds or just plant bad luck.

Being aware of companion planting means you can deliberately put plants that help each other together while separating out plants that do not play together nicely. It is highly beneficial for you and means you get better quality plants every single year. Companion planting removes a lot of the guess work from growing a good crop of vegetables.

If you live in an area which is afflicted with certain pests or diseases, then use companion planting to help reduce the impact of these problems. They may not solve the problem completely, but they will go a long way to reducing the negative effect on your plants.

Companion planting is completely organic, and so appeals to a lot of people who want to look after the environment and minimize their use of chemicals. When done properly you can significantly reduce your reliance on artificial chemicals while improving your yield.

For many gardeners, companion planting is a hotly debated subject. You have one camp that is firm in their stance that companion planting is nothing but a placebo developed by hippies. The other group attest that companion works and is the best thing ever.

In my opinion, companion planting works, but like everything else, should not be blindly followed or believed. It does work when done correctly and certainly doesn't cause any problems. Most companion planting is a combination of science and common sense.

The planting of marigolds with tomatoes is perhaps a good example of this. This pairing is done because it keeps nematodes away. However, what you may not be aware of is that marigolds only work on certain types of nematodes and only certain types of marigolds work. Also, the effect is cumulative, so you may not get much protection in the first year as it can take several years for the chemicals produced by the marigolds to build up in the soil to a level where they are effective against nematodes.

There are numerous benefits to companion planting, including:

- Attracting Insects – many companion plants attract beneficial insects such as bees for pollination or ladybugs (ladybirds) to eat aphids and so on
- Shelter – larger plants as companions can provide shelter from rain, the wind or even too much sun
- Soil Improvement – some plants, such as beans, fix nitrogen into the soil which can then be used by other plants
- Support – as per the three sisters method, some plants provide support for climbing plants
- Decoy Plants – some plants act as a decoy, either the insects attack them instead of your crop (such as planting roses with grape vines), or they mask the presence of your crop with its smell, such as planting leeks or onions with your carrots to deter carrot fly.

One thing to also consider is that there are also antagonist plants as well as companion plants, i.e. Plants which stunt the growth of each other when planted together. A good example is black walnut trees, which release a chemical into the soil which prevents other plants from growing near it.

When you start companion planting you will realize how growing a monoculture, which most of us do, where plants are grown in rows of or blocks of a single species, actively encourages pests and diseases. With companion planting you plant other plants in the same row, they can still be productive vegetables, but they also reduce the incidence of pests and diseases.

Filling your garden full of herbs will also help repel pests, attract bees and they are fantastic in your cooking! You will learn later about the various herbs you can grow as companions and which plants the different herbs work best with.

Intercropping is another great way to maximize your use of space. In the same row in between your slow growing vegetables, such as cabbage and cauliflower, you sow fast-growing vegetables such as lettuce or radishes. This maximizes your use of space as well as helping to keep down weeds. In some cases, this can provide companion planting benefits.

There are lots and lots of different types of companion planting, and even the dreaded weed can be your friend, in certain circumstances. This technique is good fun, helps you get the most from your vegetable garden, and most importantly, keeps pests and diseases to a minimum. You can even plant green manures, which are turned into the soil to build it up and prepare it for the next season's crop.

Once you start companion planting, you will love it. It brings a boring, straight-rowed vegetable plot to life and makes it more interesting and productive. It reduces your reliance on chemicals and helps you to work in harmony with nature.

Benefits of Companion Planting

Companion planting is receiving a lot of attention from the scientific community because it can help reduce the need for harmful chemicals in farming. Home gardeners are re-discovering this information and using it to their benefit.

There are several different ways in which companion planting can help you, including:

- *Pest Repellent* – certain plants give off chemicals either from their leaves, flowers or roots which will repel or suppress pests, protecting its neighbors. Some pests spread diseases, but keeping the bugs under control will help prevent those diseases taking over your plot. A lot of gardeners will use chemicals to control pests, so this natural pest control is more in line with organic gardening methods and helps reduce your need for chemical sprays. Catnip, for example, can repel aphids, ants, and weevils, but also keeps mice away, but not just because it attracts cats. It can take as long as a year or two for natural chemicals to build up in the soil to provide this defense, as is the case with marigolds, which deter nematodes. Some people will claim that companion planting doesn't work purely because they've not given the plants enough time to work their magic.

- *Nitrogen Fixers* – beans, clover, peas and some other plants have nodules on the roots which grow Rhizobium bacteria. These helpful bacteria take nitrogen from the atmosphere and fix it into the soil in a form that can be used by plants. This nitrogen fixing also benefits neighboring plants as well as later crops planted in the same location.
- *Sacrificial Planting* – if you have a plant that is particularly susceptible to a pest, you plant another plant nearby that the pests prefer as a decoy. The pests flock to that plant, rather than your vegetable crop. You will still get some pests on your vegetables, but not as many. Most of them will be on the sacrificial plant and can then be easily disposed of. Collard greens planted near cabbage keeps the diamondback moth away as they are more attracted to the greens. Mustard is another trap crop as it attracts cabbage worms (caterpillars) and harlequin bugs, which are extremely destructive to everything from cabbages to radishes for beetroot and potatoes, to mention just a few. Don't pull the mustard up to dispose of the harlequin bugs because they will fall off and make their way to other plants. Dunk the stems (by bending them) into soapy water, so the bugs drown. Plant mustard with clover or dill to attract parasitic wasps, which will prey on the harlequin bugs.

- *Enhancing Flavor* – some pairings will improve the flavor of your vegetable crop. One of the best-known examples of this is the pairing of basil and tomatoes. These work fantastically in the kitchen, but when grown together, the basil makes the tomatoes more flavorsome. Many herbs, when grown with vegetables, improve their flavor. German chamomile (wild chamomile) improves the flavor and growth of onions, cabbages, and cucumbers.

- *Camouflage* - a lot of pests use smell to find your precious crops or they look for the shape of your plant. By choosing companion plants with a strong smell, you can confuse many pests. For those pests that hunt by sight, companion plants can confuse the shape of the plant too.
- *Shading* – known as stacking in permaculture or as level interactions, this is the principle of planting taller plants so that they provide shelter and shade for more delicate plants. This relies on you knowing the path of the sun through the sky. One example of this is the three sisters method of planting where the corn provides welcome shade for the squash plants.
- *Attracting Beneficial Insects* – your garden needs pollinators as well as pest predators such as hoverflies, lacewings, spiders, parasitic wasps, predatory mites, and ladybirds. Planting the right companion plants will attract insects, which will keep the problem pests down and pollinate your vegetable plants. Creating the right environment for these beneficial insects will encourage them to spend their entire life-cycle in your vegetable garden. This is more important than you may think because it is the larvae of many insects that devour problem pests.
- *Increasing Biodiversity* – a good mix of plants creates a much more resilient ecosystem. Pests, adverse weather conditions, and diseases will not wipe out your entire crop, but instead just damage a portion of it, and even that can be minimized with the right planting.

Companion planting has a lot of benefits, and it is something that many more gardeners can benefit from. In this book, you will learn how you can use companion planting in your vegetable garden and increase your yields while decreasing your work. It doesn't take up extra space and doesn't detract from your main crops. It means your plants are healthier, grow better and can taste much nicer.

History of Companion Planting

The history of companion planting is not particularly known as it isn't very well documented. There are stories and oral traditions from cultures all over the world, but the origins are not clear.

The three sisters method of growing corn, squash, and beans is thought to date back thousands of years to when humans first inhabited the Americas. In China, mosquito ferns have been planted with rice crops to fix nitrogen for at least a thousand years.

As the organic culture became more popular in the late 1960's and 1970's, so companion planting also grew in popularity as a natural method of gardening. For many home gardeners, reducing the requirement for chemicals can only be a good thing, and it benefits the environment and wildlife too.

Companion planting is considered a traditional practice when growing fruit and vegetables on a smaller scale, typically used by the backyard gardener or allotmenteer. In the last thirty to forty years though, it has developed as a practice used in larger scale operations, which includes intercropping.

With a strong focus from the scientific community on improving food production while promoting sustainable farming practices, companion planting is gaining ground as scientists conclude what we've been saying for years … it works!

In more modern times, companion planting became better known in 1943 when Richard B Gregg published a pamphlet entitled "Companion Plants and How to Use Them". Around twenty years later he published a book on the subject which included the results of his own experiments as well as laboratory experiments performed by Dr. Ehrenfried Pfeiffer.

Choosing Companion Plants

Like vegetables, companion plants have requirements for their growing environment. Some are frost hardy; some are not; some prefer free-draining soil, some do not; some prefer full sun, some prefer partial or full shade. Even the growing conditions between your garden and the garden next door can be different due to micro-climates and shading. How far north or south you live has a significant impact on what companion plants you can grow, just as it does on the vegetables you can successfully grow.

You need to understand your garden. Where does the sun rise? How does it track across your garden? What obstructions cast shade? What areas rarely get any sun? What areas are sheltered? Do some areas of your garden get wetter than others?

Understanding these mini-ecosystems within your garden will help you not only correctly plant your vegetables, but also ensure you plant the best companions for them.

When you have this knowledge of the environment in your vegetable garden, you can start choosing which of the many companion plants are best suited to your specific growing area.

Most plants that you buy will give you an idea of how hardy they are and when they can be planted. Plants bought in the USA will typically show something called the hardiness zone that the plant can survive on. This gives you an idea of how far north this plant will survive through the winter months. Always bear in mind that this is a rough figure and will depend on a lot of seasonal variations. Sometimes the plant will survive a mild winter in your area, but alternatively, a freak cold winter in a warmer area will kill it off. This is where the knowledge of your environment pays off because you know the weather patterns and what is considered normal where you live.

The United States and Canada are divided into eleven planting zones, each differentiated by a 10-degree Fahrenheit difference in the average minimum temperature. The higher the number, the warmer the area. Southern Florida, for example, is in the USDA zones 9 through to 11 whereas the Northern USA and Canada are zones 1 through to 3.

Plants bought in the USA will tell you which hardiness zones they can survive in outside, but remember this is a guideline and the weather doesn't always oblige and stick to those averages.

For those of us outside of the USA, we have to use our best judgment and knowledge built up over the years. Whenever I am unsure about when something should be planted, I will ask one of the older folk on my allotment site, and they will give me a low down on the weather, microclimate, and the best time to plant anything. Alternatively, most seed packets will give you a guideline for when to sow indoors or outdoors and plant out. But please remember these are guidelines and need to be followed with some common sense. If it says plant out in April, but it isn't frost hardy then don't plant it out in April if there is snow on the ground! The weather appears far more changeable now than in the past, and you need to adjust your planting times accordingly.

A greenhouse, polytunnel or cold frame can help more tender plants survive in the colder weather. You can fleece or bubble wrap some plants to protect them from frosts, but this isn't going to work in the coldest winters.

Planting tender plants against a wall helps them to survive as the wall absorbs heat, reflecting it back to the plants. The temperature near a wall, particularly a heated house wall, tends to be a couple of degrees warmer than elsewhere outside, which can be enough for a more delicate plant to survive.

I often extend my growing seasons by fleecing delicate plants. Squash plants do not survive in a frost, yet last year my butternut squashes weren't quite ripe, so as the cold weather drew in I covered them with fleece. It protected them for several weeks before hard frosts hit and allowed the fruit to ripen fully (they were the best butternut squashes I had ever eaten by the way). I use small plastic polytunnels or up-ended plastic bottles with the bottom cut off to protect younger plants in the spring from late frosts. The longer you grow in an area, the more you will understand the vagrancies of the weather and the different micro-climates within your vegetable garden.

As well as all of this, how much light different areas of your garden gets will influence what you can plant. Some plants require full sun, which translates to a minimum of six hours of direct sunlight, not just light, but the sun directly on the plant, every single day. Partial sun or semi-shade are plants which don't mind a little bit of shade, often filtered by trees or fences. They need some direct sun but do not need it continuously. Full shade plants need light but do not appreciate direct sunlight. They are happy under trees, in the shade of fences or on the north side of a house.

The type of soil you have also influences what you can grow, both in the soil pH, soil type and nutrient levels in the soil. Some vegetable plants will grow in very specific soils, and you can only plant companions that have the same soil requirements. Of course, you can always plant companions in pots, so they have the right soil for their needs. The same applies for water requirements – plants that require differing needs will not grow successfully together.

Choosing the right companion plants for your vegetables will depend upon the specific environment you are growing in. What works for me may not work for you because our gardens and environments are different. Many of the pairings you are going to learn about will work well together as the companion plants are grown in pots (basil, mint and lemon balm being three prime examples). A lot of the companion plants detailed here are fairly hardy and tolerant of soil conditions, particularly those that are more closely related to weeds.

Companion planting isn't complex, but you do need to be aware of your own environment so that you can plant the best possible companion and get excellent results. With companion planting, you can naturally control pests, attract pollinating insects all while caring for the environment.

Companion Planting With Vegetables

Vegetables benefit significantly from companion planting. Depending on the vegetable, the companion plant can improve flavor, increase yield, protect it from pests or ward of disease. Do remember that although companion works, is it not necessarily the same in every area and for every person. Give it a go and see how it works where you live. If one of the companions doesn't have a noticeable effect in your area, then try a different one, but remember some plants can take a year or two to establish themselves and start working for you.

Asparagus
Asparagus is a great plant for the patient gardener, taking several years to establish itself fully. Planting parsley and basil in the same bed as asparagus helps the plant grow more vigorously. Tomatoes are good planted next to asparagus as they deter asparagus beetles, but also, being near the parsley and basil benefits the tomatoes by helping them grow better. Basil improves the flavor of the tomatoes and also deter tomato hornworm.

You can also plant marigolds, dill, comfrey, and coriander near asparagus. These help to deter pests such as aphids and spider mites, though be aware that some of these may not be so good for tomatoes.

Do not plant onions and garlic with asparagus as they affect its growth, as well as the growth of other plants such as peas. Potatoes should also not be planted near to asparagus either.

Beans

Beans are a great crop to plant as they fix nitrogen into the soil. Many people plant beans, harvest some of them and then dig the rest into the ground to build up the levels of nitrogen.

The most famous companion crop for beans is the three sisters method where beans, corn, and squashes are all planted together. Beans enjoy being planted with sweet corn because it provides a natural trellis.

Marigolds are great with beans because they deter the Mexican bean beetle as well as other pests. Both French and African marigolds produce a substance in their roots which helps to deter nematodes.

Potatoes and catnip are great companions as they help to deter Mexican flea beetles. Nasturtium and rosemary also help to deter flea beetles.

Summer savory should be planted near to beans, but not so close it shades them. Not only does it repel flea beetles, but it also helps to stimulate growth and improve flavor.

Cucumbers, radishes, and eggplant (aubergine) are also good companions because they encourage strong growth. Other plants that work well with beans include broccoli, cabbage, carrots, cauliflower, celery, cucumbers, peas, strawberries, and fennel. As beans fix nitrogen into the soil, the beans are very beneficial for these plants.

Do not plant beans near any member of the onion plant, including leeks, onions, garlic, or spring onions (scallions). These inhibit the growth of the beans. Also avoid planting kohlrabi, fennel, and basil near your beans for the same reason.

Beans do not get on with sunflowers, even though they are tall and should technically provide a trellis for the beans. Avoid planting the two together.

Bush and pole beans have almost all the same companion plants. There is one exception, and that is pole beans do not like being planted near beetroot (beets).

Beetroot (Beets)
As you have just learned, bush beans such as soy and butter beans make great companions for beetroot, plus they fix nitrogen into the soil for later crops. If bean beetle plagues your beans, then plant some summer savory as that will deter the beetles.

Beetroot grows well with certain members of the brassica family such as broccoli, Brussels Sprouts, cabbage, cauliflower, kale, and kohlrabi. The beetroot puts minerals into the soil that these brassicas appreciate, plus the beetroot leaves are very high in magnesium so makes a great compost for these companion plants.

Garlic makes for a very good companion for beetroot, warding off a variety of pests including root maggots, codling moths, snails, and Japanese beetles. Garlic is high in sulfur, which is a powerful anti-fungal agent that protects your beetroot from some diseases caused by fungal infections. As a companion plant, garlic improves the taste and flavor of beetroot.

Mint makes for another great companion, but it is a highly invasive plant so should only be grown in pots. Mint will improve the growth of the beetroot but also deter some pests such as aphids (by attracting predators), flea beetles, fleas, and even rodents, to a degree.

Broccoli

Broccoli doesn't like being planted with other members of the brassica family as they compete for nutrients and leave the soil in poor condition. If you are planting a bed of brassicas, then make sure you regularly feed the plants to ensure nutrient levels are kept at a sufficiently high level.

This is a very greedy plant, having a particularly high requirement for calcium. It should not be planted with other heavy feeding plants such as asparagus, sweet corn, melon, or pumpkins. Broccoli is better paired with plants that are lighter feeders. Plant beetroot, nasturtiums, radish, and similar crops with your slower growing broccoli to maximize your use of space.

Broccoli does poorly when planted with members of the nightshade family, which includes tomatoes, aubergine (eggplant), and any type of pepper, including chili, and bell. Grapes, rue, and mustard seed also have a negative effect on broccoli and should not be planted nearby. Both strawberries and pole beans also do not make good companions for broccoli.

Planting aromatic herbs such as dill, rosemary, mint (in pots), garlic, thyme, and basil near to your broccoli will help to ward off a number of harmful pests.

Other good plants include radishes, nasturtiums, marigolds, cucumber, lettuce, bush beans, and shallots. None of these compete with broccoli for nutrients and allow your main crop to pull all the calcium it needs from the soil.

Brussels Sprouts

A member of the Brassica family, Brussels Sprouts are susceptible to a wide variety of pests. They can be one of the most frustrating vegetables to grow because of the sheer number of critters that love this plant. Anything from aphids to caterpillars to whitefly and more all feel your Brussels Sprouts are a tasty snack. It is one, like all members of the brassica family, that benefits from being netted with a fine mesh net.

Nasturtiums are a great companion because they repel squash bugs, some aphids, and the annoying white fly. Basil helps to repel both flies and mosquitos but also attracts bees.

Garlic is a good companion when planted in between your Brussels Sprouts as it provides protection from aphids, Japanese beetles, and also blight. Like mint (remember to pot it), garlic improves the growth of the plant.

Marigolds are another great companion, repelling a wide variety of insects with their odor.

Mustard is a great trap crop for several insects, though once the plant has been attacked and infected, it should be removed and destroyed.

Brussels Sprouts will get on with most plants, though it does not like the company of strawberries, pole beans or tomato plants.

Cabbage
Another member of the brassica family, a number of different pests bother cabbages. Like the previous vegetable, they benefit from being netted with a fine mesh net to reduce infestations and prevent butterflies from laying their eggs on them.

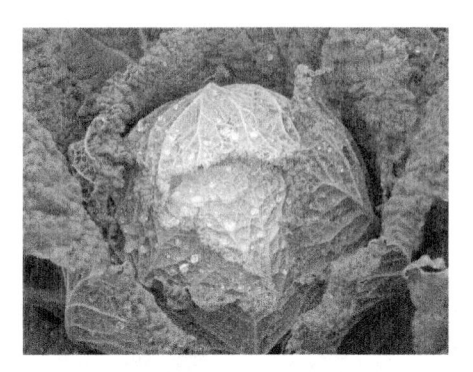

Planting with sage and rosemary, both aromatic herbs will put off cabbage moth, one of the main pests, by their strong smell. Chamomile is another great companion because it improves the flavor of the cabbage. Plant the smelly culinary herbs in between rows of cabbages and they will repel many pests plus help to keep weeds down.

Marigolds are yet another good companion for a similar reason, their scent confuses and repels pests such as aphids and cabbage moths.

Other good companions include onions, celery, and beets (beetroot) as they improve the flavor of the cabbages and repel some insects.

You should avoid planting strawberries, tomatoes, grapes, mustard, and pole beans with cabbages as they do not make good companions.

Carrots
Tomatoes are a good companion plant to carrots, though plant them around 15" apart, otherwise the tomatoes will inhibit the growth of the carrots. The tomatoes provide much needed shade for the carrots, but also secrete a chemical called solanine which kills harmful insects. The carrots break up and aerate the soil for the tomatoes, helping them to grow stronger.

One of the main pests that attack carrot is carrot flies. These destructive insects hunt by smell and can sniff out your carrots from a surprising distance. They usually fly no more than 18" above the ground and can be deterred with a fine mesh net two-foot-high around your carrots.

However, because they hunt by scent, they can be put off by aromatic plants. Interplanting your carrots with onions, garlic or leeks is enough to confuse the carrot fly's sense of smell and protect your crops. Likewise, aromatic herbs such as chives, sage, parsley, and rosemary will do exactly the same.

An often used companion is the humble radish. They are usually planted in the same row as carrots. As the carrots are very slow to germinate, the rapidly germinating radish pops it head up above the soil quickly giving you a good indicator of where your carrots are. This simple visual indicator means that you do not accidentally damage your carrots thinking they are weeds. The radishes mature and are harvested before the carrots are ready.

Beans, both bush and pole, can make a good companion when planted the year before as they fix nitrogen into the soil. Growing them with carrots though causes issues because they shade and crowd out the carrots.

To grow long, straight carrots, you should plant them in 3" wide drainpipes that are around two feet long. Fill these with a sandy soil mix and a single carrot plant put in each pipe. As carrots fork and stunt when they hit rocks or obstructions in the soil, this is the best way to get lovely long, straight carrots.

Avoid planting carrots with dill and coriander as both of these secrete a chemical from their roots which is harmful to carrots. Parsnips are also vulnerable to carrot fly so are best not planted near carrots unless you are surrounding them with protective, aromatic plants.

Cauliflower

Another member of the brassica family, cauliflowers are susceptible to a wide variety of pests. Like every other brassica, it is very susceptible to damage from the cabbage moth. It benefits from being interplanted with other crops, rather than being planted in rows as that helps to disguise your cauliflower from the cabbage moth.

Cauliflower likes high levels of nitrogen in the soil, so it is always worth planting beans in the ground before the cauliflower. A summer crop of beans, dug in to fix the nitrogen into the soil and then followed by an overwinter crop of cauliflower works particularly well.

Interplanting cauliflower with celery and oregano helps to deter a variety of pests including the dreaded cabbage moth. Cauliflower also appreciates being planted in the vicinity of tomatoes.

The one plant that doesn't do well with cauliflower is strawberries. Avoid planting these together to ensure you get the best from both plants.

Celery

Celery is an interesting plant to grow and very nice in salads and stews. Careful not to plant too many as it can be hard to use them all up and they do have a tendency to bolt if left in the ground too long.

Planting celery near any member of the cabbage family is a great idea. The scent of the celery plant deters the cabbage moth, which will then leave your brassicas alone.

Leeks and onions grow well with celery and will help prevent infestations by insects that feast on it. Planting flowers such as snapdragons, cosmos, nasturtiums, marigolds, and daisies near to your celery will also help to keep harmful pests away from your vegetable crop while attracting beneficial insects and predators such as parasitic wasps.

Bush beans and peas are a good companion because they add much needed nitrogen to the soil. Planting celery in the shade of either spinach or tomato will help to keep the sun off the celery and prevent it from drying out.

Avoid planting celery near corn or asters as these will encourage harmful pests and diseases. Also, avoid planting near potato and parsnip because these will use up all the nutrients in the soil and encourage potentially harmful insects.

Corn (Sweet Corn)

Sweet corn is a popular crop to grow, producing delicious ears of corn. Remember that it should always be planted in blocks rather than rows to encourage pollination.

Corn benefits from being planted with beans or peas as they fix nitrogen into the soil, remember the three sisters method we discussed earlier? It also benefits from being planted with any member of the squash family as this acts as a mulch to the soil, helping to retain moisture and keep weeds down.

If your area is plagued with raccoons, then interplanting corn with cucumbers will help prevent the raccoons stealing your crop. Cucumbers are unpleasant to raccoons for some reason, and they will stay away from your crops.

Clover can be planted with corn to act as a living mulch and to fix nitrogen into the soil. This isn't very popular with gardeners as clover can run amok, but one study showed that clover and corn together produced the largest and best crop of corn.

Although some people say you should plant potatoes with corn, the benefit comes in hot areas where the corn shades the potatoes, which prefer cooler weather. In most other areas, planting the two together is not a good idea because they both make high demands on nutrients in the soil at the same time. If you are feeding your crops regularly then, this will not be so much of a problem, but the competition can cause both crops to grow poorly as they use up the nutrients in the soil. Also, potatoes attract many pests that will feast on corn, including potato aphid, cutworm, fall army worm and others.

Tomatoes should not be planted near sweet corn because they attract several pests that will decimate your corn crop, including corn earworm also known as the tomato fruit worm and the tomato hornworm.

Cucumber

This is a popular crop to grow in a greenhouse, or outside in warmer areas. It is also a very thirsty plant, so does not like being planted near other plants that also need lots of water.

Spotted Cucumber Beetle

Cucumbers grow well with corn, as you just found out, and will use the corn as support while deterring raccoons. Both marigolds and nasturtiums are good planted with cucumbers as they deter harmful pests. The former is good at repelling beetles while the latter deters thrips and several other insects. Oregano also makes a good companion due to its insect repelling properties. Dill is another herb beneficial for cucumbers as it helps to improve the flavor of the ripe fruit. You can also plant lettuce, radishes, and onions near to cucumbers and they will have a beneficial effect.

Like many plants, beans and peas work well with cucumbers, particularly when grown the year before in the cucumber bed. They fix nitrogen in the soil which is highly beneficial to the cucumber plants.

Potatoes should not be planted with cucumbers because they compete for nutrients and water. Sage is an herb that should not be planted near cucumbers because it causes poor growth. Also, avoid planting tomatoes near to cucumbers as they do not grow well together.

Eggplant (Aubergine)

Eggplant, or aubergine as it is known in Europe, is a popular vegetable plant with a long growing season. In cooler areas, it must be grown under glass, yet in warmer climates where the growing season is long enough, it will grow outside.

To deter flea beetles, plant catnip, though make sure you cover this with something like chicken wire otherwise your plants will be beset by every cat in the area!

Hot peppers are another good companion as they secrete a chemical from their roots which prevent both root rot and Fusarium diseases. Sweet peppers have a similar effect but secrete slightly lower amounts of this chemical.

As with many other plants, beans make a good companion for their ability to fix nitrogen into the soil. Just be careful that your pole beans do not shade your eggplants as they like direct sun. Bush beans, however, provide a different benefit to pole beans because they repel the dreaded Colorado potato beetle. You can use Mexican marigold for its beetle repelling properties, but beans do not like it, so you'll have to choose either beans or marigolds.

French tarragon and thyme are beneficial herbs to plant with aubergine as they repel harmful insects. Thyme also has the effect of deterring garden moths.

Tomatoes also make a good companion for eggplants as do spinach and potatoes (you can buy a grafted plant that produces both potatoes and eggplants). Be careful that tomatoes do not shade eggplants but allow eggplants to shade spinach, another good companion.

Kohlrabi
Kohlrabi, coming from the German word for "cabbage turnip," is a cooler weather crop that is not commonly grown. A member of the cabbage family, it isn't particularly hardy and suffers from all the usual problems that affect brassicas.

Plant onions with your kohlrabi to deter pests. The smell puts off cabbage moth and many of the other common pests. Lettuces interplanted with kohlrabi will repel earth flies.

Kohlrabi does not like being planted with strawberries or tomatoes. Both of these will stunt its growth. Pole beans should not be planted near kohlrabi either.

Leek

As a member of the allium family, companion planting with leeks is very similar to that of onions. Although leeks, onions, and garlic will all grow well together in a single bed, you need to be careful that this type of monoculture doesn't attract pests or encourages a build-up of diseases.

Leeks grow very well with strawberries, surprisingly enough. The smell of the leek deters many of the pests which feast on strawberries. Leeks can also be grown near to apple trees where they will grow well and repel pests from the apples.

Interplanting leeks and carrots works extremely well. The odor of the leeks puts off the carrot fly, but the onion fly, a common pest on leeks, is deterred by carrots! There is the added benefit of the both break up the soil which helps them both to grow.

To protect the leeks from pests, you can plant nasturtiums, marigold, and poppies nearby. The scent of these plants puts of the pests that affect leeks. Other good companion includes celery, parsley, beetroot, and tomatoes.

Pole beans and peas should not be planted near leeks as they do not grow well together and the leeks will stunt the growth of the beans and peas. The leeks exude a compound called ajoene which, although an anti-fungal agent, is not beneficial to either peas or beans.

Lettuce
A popular crop, this is most at risk from slugs. Growing mint, in pots, and positioning it around your lettuce crop will help repel these voracious pests.

Lettuce is great to plant with onions, leeks, or carrots. As these are all slow growing crops, they often struggle to compete with the faster growing weeds. A broad leaf lettuce will grow and crowd out the weeds, leaving more room for the carrots and onions to grow. As these need more space, you harvest the lettuce, and then th ground is weed free. The same principle applies to broccoli, which also needs a lot of space between plants which weeds take over.

Radishes also grow well with lettuce as the radish grows very quickly. Plus, the lettuce helps give the radish a better flavor. A bed containing radishes, carrots, and lettuces works very well together.

Cucumber is another good companion for lettuce, though be careful it doesn't crowd out the lettuce. As radishes deter cucumber beetle, planting some of those too will help protect your cucumbers.

Another good companion plant is strawberries. These grow together well, particularly with the addition of some onions to repel pests. Marigolds also grow well with lettuce and beans or peas are good to plant before lettuce to fix nitrogen into the soil.

Avoid planting lettuce together with parsley as the two plants do not complement each other

Onions

This is a great crop to interplant with any member of the brassica family. Onions repel cabbage worms, cabbage loopers, and cabbage maggots. The strong scent of the onions puts off these pests and keeps your brassicas pest free.

Onions are also planted with carrots for a similar reason; the scent confuses the carrot fly which means you get a decent crop of carrots.

Other good companions for onions include lettuce, tomatoes, strawberries, and peppers. This is because onions also repel several other pests, including aphids, rabbits, and Japanese beetles.

Avoid planting peas, beans, asparagus, and sage with your onions. These plants do not play well with onions and hinder growth. You should also avoid planting too many onions together. Onions are affected by the onion maggot, which travels from onion to onion. If your onions are scattered over your garden, then this maggot will not travel between your onions and will just damage one or two plants rather than decimate your entire crop.

Peas

This popular crop makes for a great companion crop for a wide variety of plants. However, it doesn't grow well with any allium, including shallots, garlic, chives, and onions. Keep these away from your peas! You should also avoid planting peas near the flower gladioli as it will hinder the growth of your peas.

Planting peas with coriander (cilantro), sage, marjoram or mint (in pots) works well as these pungent herbs help deter a variety of pests. Marjoram will help attract pollinators to your peas, ensuring a bumper crop.

Other good companions for peas include radishes, carrots, parsnips, turnips, and any member of the cabbage family. Be aware that the root crops can be crowded out by peas if they are planted too close together. However, as many of these are slow growing, they are ready after the fast-growing peas mature. As you learned earlier, peas are suitable for part of the three sisters growing method, which means they grow well with beans, corn, and cucumber.

Potatoes
Potatoes are a popular crop and susceptible to a wide variety of pests and diseases. Companion planting can help organically control these problems and minimize the damage they cause. If your area is particularly susceptible to a pest or disease, then look for a potato variety that has some resistance bred into it.

Potatoes are deep rooted plants, so it makes sense that many of its companion plants are shallow rooted. As many potatoes are late season plants, early season plants such as lettuce, spinach, radish, and spring onions (scallions) make great companion plants, being harvested before the potatoes mature and crowd them out.

You can improve the flavor of your potatoes by growing basil, chamomile, parsley, thyme, and yarrow with it. These also have the additional advantage of attracting beneficial insects to your vegetable garden. Cabbage, corn, and beans all help potatoes to grow and give the resulting crop a better flavor.

To increase the resistance to disease, plant horseradish near to your potatoes. As potatoes are very susceptible to the Colorado potato beetle, plant tansy, catnip (remember to net it to prevent visits by cats) and cilantro (coriander) around your potatoes. The beetle dislikes these plants and will be repelled.

The dreaded Colorado potato beetle

Do not plant potatoes anywhere near any member of the nightshade family, including peppers, tomatoes, and eggplant (aubergine). As potatoes themselves are a member of this family, planting other members nearby will increase the risk of pests and diseases. Both tomatoes and potatoes are susceptible to blight, and it will transfer from one to the other. Keep these crops well separated to prevent the transmission of blight. Ideally, do not plant another member of the nightshade family in the same soil for two years to ensure that pests and diseases do not build up in the soil.

There are a few other plants you should not plant near your potatoes as they increase the risk of blight, including raspberries, squashes, cucumbers, pumpkins, and sunflowers.

Asparagus, turnips, fennel, and onions should not be planted with potatoes as they stunt their growth.

Flowers that make good companions for potatoes include petunias, marigold, and nasturtium.

Pumpkin

Pumpkins are a fun plant to grow, though they take up a lot of space. Because they can grow so big, they do not make for good companions for most plants. They tend to crowd out other plants due to the speed with which they grow once established.

However, pumpkins can be planted with corn and beans using the three sisters method. Be aware that your corn needs to be at least two feet tall before you put the pumpkins in the ground otherwise the pumpkins will crowd out the corn and kill it off. In the three sisters method, the pumpkin is the last plant to go in the ground because of its speedy growth.

Do not plant pumpkins near to potatoes as they will increase the risk of potato blight.

Spinach

Spinach is a great crop where you can harvest the young leaves as and when you need them for use in a salad. They appreciate some shade so you can plant them in the shadow of taller plants such as beans or peas.

Spinach can also be planted with lettuce and strawberries, both of which encourage healthy growth.

The main problem that you will encounter with spinach will be slugs and snails. These can be prevented either by growing a sacrificial crop, growing mint, scattering torn mint leaves or using any other methods of control.

Squashes

Squashes, including zucchini (courgette), have the same companion plants as pumpkins but will work well under fruit trees and with strawberries. They are most famous as part of the three sisters growing method.

Icicle radishes are great companions to squashes. Plant several radishes with your squash plant, and it will deter several pests including cucumber beetles and squash bugs.

Nasturtiums also make good companions, improving the taste and growth of the squash plants. According to a study by the North Dakota State University, nasturtiums also help repel pests such as aphids. Marigolds make for a good companion because it too will repel a variety of pests.

Radishes are another good companion for its pest repelling properties. Herbs such as catmint, dill, peppermint, oregano, marjoram, parsley, mint, and lemon balm all help repel insects. Remember that mint and lemon balm must be kept in pots otherwise they will spread like wildfire and take over your vegetable garden.

Avoid planting squashes with pumpkins because they will attract pests and diseases, increasing the risk of losing your crop. Also, avoid planting near to potatoes because they too are greedy plants and the competition for nutrients will stunt the growth of both plants.

Strawberries

Another very popular plant to grow at home, strawberries are susceptible to a wide variety of pests and diseases, meaning companion planting is very welcome. One of your biggest problems will be slugs and snails, so use the usual controls to keep these off your crop. They also benefit from being netted as birds are rather partial to fresh strawberries and will decimate your crop given half a chance.

Most flowering plants make good companions for strawberries as they attract pollinators and beneficial insects. Borage is a popular companion not only for its flowers (which are also edible), but because it repels unwanted pests. Yarrow, evening primrose, goldenrod and Roman chamomile also attract beneficial insects to your strawberry crop.

Catnip is another good companion, though remember to cover it to prevent cats wrecking your main crop. This will repel aphids and cabbage loopers, both major pests for the strawberry. Rue is another good plant to grow which will repel beetles while basil repels both mites and aphids.

Lettuce is a popular companion plant for strawberries, and the two grow very well together. Beans and peas also make for good companions because they add nitrogen to the soil, which the strawberries appreciate.

Onions and garlic are excellent companions for strawberries as their strong smell repels several harmful insects. Spinach also makes for a good neighbor because it exudes compounds called saponins which repel many of the pests that feed on strawberries.

Strawberries can be planted with blueberries and cranberries. All three plants like a slightly acidic soil, plus the strawberries will act as a mulch for the shrub berries, keeping weeds down and helping the soil to retain moisture.

Strawberries should not be planted near cabbages or broccoli due to them being susceptible to many similar pests.

Tomatoes

One of the most popular crops grown at home, tomatoes are also one of the most frustrating due to the sheer number of pests and diseases that can affect them. Being such a commonly grown crop, there is a lot of knowledge about companion planting relating to tomato plants.

Basil is one of the best companion plants for tomatoes, and this herb is delicious when served with tomatoes. Not only does basil improve the health of the plant and the taste of the fruit, but it also repels numerous insects, including whiteflies, spider mites, aphids, and hornworms. For best results, plant three basil plants for each tomato bush about 10" away, planting in a pattern, so each basil plant serves multiple tomato plants.

Borage is another great herb to plant with tomatoes. It improves both the flavor of the fruit and the health of the plant but also repels the hornworm and cabbage worm.

Planting chives near your tomatoes will help repel aphids while attracting pollinating insects. Garlic will also repel spider mites, and many people will bury garlic cloves around their tomato plants to repel insects.

French marigolds are often planted with tomatoes as they deter nematodes, slugs, tomato worm, and several other pests. For best results, these need to be grown for a couple of years to build up protection in the soil. At the end of the growing season, turn the spent marigolds into the soil and let them break down naturally to enhance their nematode repellent properties.

Mint makes for a good companion, but ensure it is grown in containers because it is very invasive. Mint will deter a number of pests, including rodents, fleas, aphids, flea beetles, ants, and white cabbage moths.

Nasturtiums are worth planting with your tomatoes as they will deter whiteflies, aphids, beetles, squash bugs, and ward of fungal infections.

One particularly beneficial herb is parsley, purely because it attracts hover flies, which are a beneficial predator.

Tomatoes and asparagus make for an excellent companion because asparagus repels nematodes and tomatoes return the compliment by repelling the asparagus beetle.

Carrots work well when planted with tomatoes because they help break up the soil, which the tomatoes appreciate. Also, in many cases, the carrots will be ready to harvest before the tomatoes have grown large enough to crowd them out. Likewise, spinach makes for an excellent companion as it is ready to harvest before the tomatoes grow too large.

You should avoid planting any member of the cabbage family near tomatoes. These do not make good companions and will inhibit the growth of your tomatoes.

Corn is another crop to avoid planting near tomatoes as they share several common pests such as the tomato fruit worm and corn earworm. Fennel should also be avoided because it inhibits the growth of tomatoes.

Potatoes should not be planted near tomatoes as both suffer from blight and it will transfer from one crop to the other. There are blight resistant varieties of both potatoes and tomatoes, though this doesn't mean they are immune. If you do suffer from blight, destroy all infected plant material and pick up all leaf debris from the soil to reduce the risk of blight the following year.

Dill is a bit of an odd companion for tomatoes because when it is young, it will help the tomatoes grow and improve their health. As the dill matures it will stunt the growth of the tomatoes. If you are growing dill near your tomatoes, harvest it before it matures.

Tomatoes are good companions for rose bushes. Interplanted amongst roses, they will protect them from black spot. Tomatoes planted near gooseberries will repel harmful insects.

Turnips (Rutabaga)

Peas make an excellent companion for turnips because they fix nitrogen into the soil, which the turnips appreciate.

Cabbages and turnips make for excellent companions because the turnips repel many pests which feast on cabbages. Turnips are also known to repel aphids and so make a good companion crop for any plant that suffers from aphid infestations.

Root vegetables, potatoes, radishes, and mustard do not make good companions for turnips as they compete for nutrients.

Zucchini (Courgette)

Radishes make for an excellent companion for zucchini because they repel several harmful pests, including cucumber beetles, squash bugs, and aphids. Interplant the radishes with your zucchini plant and sow throughout the growing season.

Interplanting garlic with your zucchini will also help to repel aphids. Beans and peas are a popular companion due to their ability to fix nitrogen into the soil.

Both nasturtiums and marigolds are excellent companion plants. The former act as a sacrificial crop, attracting aphids and flea beetles away from your precious vegetables. The marigolds repel a wide variety of pests with the aroma they produce. Of course, both plants flower profusely, which means they attract pollinators which benefit your zucchini plants.

There are several herbs to plant near zucchini to repel pest and attract beneficial insects, including borage, parsley, mint, marjoram, lemon balm, dill, oregano, catnip, and peppermint.

If you plant zucchini around the base of your corn plants, then it will confuse the squash vine borer.

Avoid planting potatoes in the vicinity of zucchini or any squash plant because they will inhibit their growth.

COMPANION PLANTING WITH FLOWERS

Companion planting is a fantastic way to naturally protect your plants from a wide variety of pests and diseases. You have already learned that by siting certain vegetables together, you can protect your valuable crops from harm. You will have read about some of the flowers that act as companions, with both marigolds and nasturtiums coming up repeatedly as excellent companion plants.

Flowers are a wonderful addition to your vegetable garden. Not only do they add a lovely splash of color, but they also encourage a wide variety of beneficial insects that prey on other insects that will cause your vegetables harm, as well as attracting pollinators.

When companion planting with flowers you need to consider a few factors.

When do the flowers bloom? If your aim is to attract pollinators, then you need to ensure that the flowers are in full bloom at the same time as your vegetable plants otherwise pollination will not occur.

Also, consider the growing conditions of the flowers. They need to be positioned with plants that have similar soil, water, and sunlight requirements. Make sure that your flowers do not grow too tall and overshadow your vegetable crops, denying them vital sunlight.

Of course, if you want to express your artistic side, then you can pair flowers with vegetables where the shapes and colors complement each other. This can turn a stark vegetable garden into a beautiful yet productive display.

Flowers tend to fall into one of three categories:

- Annuals
- Biennials
- Perennials

Annual flowers will complete a full life cycle within a year, i.e. They grow, flower and seed all in a single growing season. There are also hardy annuals which can be sown before winter to sprout in the spring.

Biennials have a two-year life cycle, basil being a good example of this type of plant. A biennial will flower in its first year of growth, then flower and seed in their second year.

Perennial flowers are cold hardy to a degree, some more so than others. These will die back every winter and then re-grow in the spring. These are ideal for the borders of your vegetable garden as they will attract predators and pollinators. Some good perennial flowers include hollyhocks, helenium, astrantia, and penstemon.

Which flowers you grow will depend on where you live, what vegetables you grow and what flowers you like. I tend to grow a lot of flowering herbs such as chives, oregano, and marjoram, but also have flowers such as nasturtiums growing around the outside of my vegetable plot. Others, such as marigolds are planted throughout the vegetable garden where required.

Here are some of the most popular and best companion flowers:

Calendula
Also known as pot marigold, this differs from the other type of marigolds we will talk about shortly. This is an easy to grow plant and will flower throughout the year, particularly if you remove the seed heads. The seeds

can easily be dried and stored for the following year.

Calendula are a member of the daisy family and are an edible flower, though it is somewhat bitter. It has a very bright orange color. This helpful plant will repel pests such as the tomato hornworm and asparagus beetle but will attract aphids. It is very helpful as a trap crop, planted on one side of your garden to attract aphids away from your vegetable crops.

Marigolds

These are very commonly found in the vegetable garden as they attract insects and are a superb companion plant. Many serious vegetable producers grow large amounts of marigolds every year because they are so useful as companions.

Marigolds grow in pretty much any soil and are available in a wide variety of colors, though most commonly seen with yellow blooms. The French marigold is very popular because it produces a chemical that deters nematodes, though it can take several years for this to build up to a suitable level in the soil. At the end of the growing season, leave the roots in the soil and just turn the foliage under the soil where it will break down.

Marigolds are a great companion plant for a wide variety of vegetables, in particular for melons where they help to deter nematodes.

If you plant marigolds around your vegetable garden, then they will deter rabbits. Planting marigolds with your bean plants will deter Mexican bean beetles. They are also known to repel thrips, whiteflies, tomato hornworms, and squash bugs, making them an ideal companion for many vegetable plants.

Chamomile and Daisy

These plants are very good at attracting a wide variety of beneficial insects, including hoverflies and predatory wasps. Chamomile is great to grow because the leaves make a popular herbal tea.

An alternative use for chamomile tea is as a spray to prevent damping off (a fungal disease) on seedlings.

Chamomile stores magnesium, potassium, and calcium, so can be dug into the soil at the end of the growing season to build up these micro-nutrients in the ground. As chamomile is best kept clipped to prevent it become leggy, the clippings can be spread around the base of any plant to give it a boost.

The scent of chamomile is also known to deter mosquitos.

Comfrey

Comfrey is considered a weed by many gardeners, but it does have its uses. Be aware that it has long, deep roots that are very brittle and it will grow back from even the smallest piece of root. If you are growing comfrey, then you should grow it in containers because it is so invasive.

Bees absolutely love comfrey as it is full of flowers in the summer time and will flock to this plant. The leaves make for an excellent mulch for your plants that is full of nutrients. The leaves are also used to make a compost tea that is very nutritious for your plants.

Nasturtiums

These are a lovely flower that produces a bright display every summer. It is a very useful plant as you can eat the flowers and the leaves, which have a slightly peppery taste and the seeds, when pickled become capers, which are an expensive delicacy.

Nasturtiums don't so particularly attract beneficial insects, but it does act as a trap or sacrificial crop. Blackfly or aphids are very attracted to nasturtiums and will usually leave your main crops alone to flock to this plant. It is then very easy to remove the affected stems and dispose of them.

This helpful plant also provides some protection from both squash bugs and beetles. The seeds are quite large and very easy to collect and keep for the following season, though you will usually find that they self-seed. Plant these amongst your cucumbers to provide protection against cucumber beetles.

Cosmos

These are a very easy to grow annual plant that produces a wonderful display of color. In your vegetable garden, plant either the bright orange or the white varieties as these attract not only bees, but also green lacewings. These delicate looking insects are surprisingly good predators and feast on many of the soft-bodied insects, such as scale insects, thrips, and aphids, that can be found on your vegetable plants.

Sweet Peas

These are another beautiful crop that produces a wash of color. There are hundreds of different varieties on the market from dwarf to full size in a wide range of colors.

Plant sweet peas with your pole beans for a wonderful wash of color, plus they will attract beneficial pollinators to your plants.

Roses

Although roses don't make a particularly good companion plant, they are helpful when planted near grape vines as they attract aphids. When you see aphids on your roses, you know to protect your vines. Many grapevine growers will use roses as a trap crop to protect the precious grapes.

Roses, though, are affected by a wide variety of pests. Planting garlic near your rose bushes will help deter a lot of these pests. Garlic chives also have a similar effect but has the added benefit of producing a lovely display of flowers.

Green Manures

Green manures are incredibly useful to grow, usually being sown towards the end of summer or autumn. The idea is that it locks nutrients into the soil, preventing them from being washed away in the winter rains. The following spring, the green manure is dug back into the soil where it breaks down and releases the nutrients back into the soil. A green manure can help prevent soil being washed away by rain and provide a habitat for beneficial insects.

If you have a bare patch of ground over winter or even space between crops or plants, then a green manure can be used to fill that space. Mustard, for example, grows very quickly and if planted by mid-September will be ready to be dug into the soil in October, or you can leave it to be killed off by frost and become a mulch.

There is summer grown green manures too, including fenugreek and buckwheat. These have very dense foliage that is an effective weed suppressant. Many gardeners will plant green manure rather than cover growing beds because they can add nutrients back to the soil.

Another type of green manure are the legumes, which are members of the pea and bean family. The advantage of these, which I am sure you are aware of by now, is that they fix nitrogen into the soil which your next crop will benefit from.

I would not recommend planting a green manure in a bed where you don't have the weeds under control. If the area is infested with mares tail, bindweed or any other weed that spreads from its roots, then you can end up digging these weeds in and spreading them around. Remove all perennial weeds from the ground before planting green manure to ensure you get the most from it.

Using Green Manures
Green manures are usually sown in rows or scattered over the soil. When you are ready to use that area, cut down the foliage and leave it for a few days to wilt. Then dig both the roots and the foliage into the top 10-12 inches of the soil.

Once you have dug in the green manure, leave the area for a minimum of two weeks before planting. Using the area too early can cause problems for your plants as the decaying green manure can hamper growth.

Be aware that a thick carpet of green manure can provide a haven for slugs and snails, so you may need to take extra preventative measures against these pests if you are growing vegetable nearby.

Types of Green Manure
There are a lot of different types of green manure and which you use will depend on several factors, including:

- What time of year you are sowing the green manure
- How long you are leaving the green manure in place
- Whether you want to fix nitrogen into the soil or suppress weeds

Choose the best green manure for your needs. Green manure seeds can be bought online or you can find them in large garden stores.

Alfalfa (Medicago sativa)
This is a member of the league family and can be dug into the soil after just two or three months. In larger areas, it can be left for a year or two before being dug in. Farmers often use alfalfa as a green manure for fallow fields.

Alfalfa is best sown between April and July and is ideal for alkaline soils. Some alfalfa seeds are injected with nitrogen fixing bacteria and so can be used to fix nitrogen into the soil. Normal alfalfa seeds will not fix nitrogen into the soil.

Alsike Clover (Trifolium hybridum)
Another legume, this can be dug in after two or three months or, in larger areas, left for up to two years. It grows well in wet or acidic soils and is typically sown from April through to August.

Bitter Blue Lupin (Lupinus angustifolius)
This is a perennial flower, also a member of the legume family. It grows very well in soils that are light, sandy, or acidic. This is best sown between March and June, usually being left for two or three months before it is dug in.

Buckwheat (Fagopyrum esculentum)
This is a half-hardy annual plant that grows in spring and summer, usually sown between April and August. It grows very well in nutrient poor soils and is dug in after two or three months.

Crimson Clover (Trifolium incarnatum)
This perennial legume grows well in a light soil. It is sown anytime from March through to August, typically being dug in after two or three months. However, you can leave this green manure in the ground up until it flowers.

Essex Red Clover (Trifolium pratense)

A great perennial green manure that is ideal for loamy soils. It is sown between March and August, being dug in after two or three months or left for up to two years if required.

Fenugreek (Trigonella foenum-graecum)

An annual legume which is planted in the spring or summer. In the UK, it doesn't fix nitrogen into the soil but does in warmer climates. It is typically dug in after two or three months.

Grazing Rye (Seale cereale)

This green manure is ideal to improve soil structure and will overwinter well in most areas. It is sown anytime between August and November, being dug in the next spring.

Mustard (Sinpalis alba)
An annual crop that is a member of the brassica family, therefore should not be followed by any other brassica as it could encourage the build-up of clubroot disease. This is sown between March and September, being dug in after two or three months.

Phacelia (Phacelia tanacetifolia)
In milder areas, this green manure with very pretty flowers will overwinter and can be sown in the autumn months. Typically, though, it is planted between April and August, being dug in after two or three months.

Trefoil (Medicago lupulina)

This legume will overwinter well and can either be an annual or biennial plant. It prefers a light, dry soil that is alkaline and is sown between March and August. Trefoil can be dug in after two or three months or can be left for up to two years in larger areas.

Winter Field Bean (Vicia faba)

An annual legume that is ideal for heavy soils. Sown between September and November, it can be dug in anytime from two months after sowing up until when it flowers.

Winter Tares (Vicia sativa)

A hardy legume that will overwinter well, even in a heavy soil. Sown any time from March to August, it can be dug in two or three months later. For overwintering, sow between July and September.

Jason Johns

Companion Planting With Herbs

Herbs are very popular for the home gardener. They are great for cooking and can be dried or frozen for use in the winter months. Most gardeners will have a few herbs in their vegetable plot, but herbs can be very valuable as companion plants, which justifies growing them in larger quantities.

Here are some of the more common herbs together with their uses as a companion plant and in the kitchen. I have a variety of herbs that are kept on my allotment, being grown amongst my vegetables or in my greenhouse. I also have pots of herbs right outside my kitchen door, not for companion planting, but purely for cooking. It is wonderful to grab a handful of fresh herbs to add flavor to a dish.

Anise (Pimpinella anisum)
Anise is an unusual herb, which is less popular now than it used to be. It produces lacy, white flowers on stems that can grow up to three feet tall. As it is a tall plant, be careful not to plant it where it can cast shade on other plants.

Plant this together with either coriander or beans to promote their growth. When planted with coriander it will improve germination. Avoid planting near basil, beans, or rue as they do not grow well together.

Anise will attract predatory wasps and other beneficial insects to your garden. It is also believed to deter biting insects such as lice.

In the kitchen, anise makes for a great spice to use in cakes, cookies, and bread. It is also delicious served with any spaghetti dish, shellfish, or cottage cheese.

Basil (Ocimum basilicum)

Basil is probably one of the most commonly used herbs both in the kitchen and as a companion plant. It is easy to grow and loves a warm environment with plenty of sun, making it ideal for growing in a greenhouse. Be aware that it is a thirsty plant and will dry out easily. In cooler climates, it is an annual, though in warmer areas it is a biennial plant. If you live in a cooler area, grow basil in pots and bring it inside during the coldest months and it can survive the winter.

Basil makes a great companion for a wide variety of vegetables, including asparagus, beans, beetroot, cabbage, chili plants, bell peppers, aubergines (eggplant), oregano, potatoes, marigolds, and, of course, tomatoes.

Tomatoes are one of the most common plants that are grown with basil, usually together in a greenhouse. These two plants work together well in the kitchen, but when planted together also help improve the flavor of both plants.

Planting basil with chamomile helps basil plants grow faster and stronger. Avoid planting sage and rue with basil as they hamper its growth.

Basil grows well with anise as it helps increase oil production within the basil.

One of the benefits of basil is that, when it flowers, it will attract butterflies into your garden. It is said to repel several insects including aphids, whiteflies, asparagus beetles, tomato hornworms and mosquitoes. According to some experts, basil slows the growth of the milkweed bug.

Of course, basil is best known for its use in the kitchen, where it is great in any tomato dishes, most Italian dishes, pesto, sauces, and salads. If using it fresh, stir it into your dish just before serving to get the most taste.

Borage (Borago officinalis)

Borage is a popular plant for companion planting, not least because it produces a lot of flowers which attract pollinating insects and predatory wasps. As well as this, it is useful in the kitchen. The leaves go well in a salad and the flowers, which have a slightly spicy taste, are great in stews or soups. Pregnant and nursing women should avoid eating borage though as it isn't good for them.

Borage makes an excellent companion for your tomatoes and cabbages. It repels both the tomato worm and the cabbage worm, both of which can be huge problems for the home grower. It also has a good reputation for improving the flavor of strawberries as well as being a good companion for many different herbs.

One of the big advantages of this plant is that it adds trace minerals to the soil, with the leaves being very high in Vitamin C, calcium, and potassium. Borage leaves make for a very nutritious mulch for any of your plants and is also great to add to your compost bin.

Caraway (Carum carvi)

Caraway is a bit of an unusual herb to grow, though the seeds are occasionally used in the kitchen, particularly for rye bread and soups. This herb is great used in salads, coleslaw, over pork or even in applesauce!

Caraway grows a very long taproot which is perfect for breaking up and conditioning your soil. Anyone who suffers from a heavy soil should look at planting caraway in empty spaces to help loosen up the soil. It grows very well with most herbs, though avoid planting it with either dill or fennel as they will kill the caraway plant. As a biennial plant, mark where it is planted, so you don't accidentally plant a poor companion near to it the following spring.

Due to its long roots, it is a great companion for most shallow rooted plants, strawberries being one its best partners. However, it does make a good companion for any berry plant. It is also a beneficial companion for peas.

This plant will attract parasitic wasps and flies to your garden, which will help keep pests down on your vegetable crop.

Catnip (Nepeta cataria)

Catnip is best known for as the drug of choice for cats, working on all felines from your cat at home to the big cats such as lions and tigers. As well as this, it is an excellent companion plant in your garden. However, as it does draw the cats in, you should always cage catnip when it is planted near your vegetables to prevent curious cats from damaging your crops.

Catnip is a great companion for all members of the squash family, including pumpkins as well as for beetroot. Hyssop and catnip grow very well together, with both producing pleasant light blue flowers. It is also a good companion for tomatoes and collards.

This plant will attract pollinating insects to your garden. It works to repel several pests from your garden including aphids, ants, flea beetles, cockroaches, squash bugs, weevils, and Japanese beetles. It is also very good at repelling both rats and mice. Plant catnip around any plant that is susceptible to these pests. Tests have also shown that catnip repels the Colorado potato beetle, making it an ideal companion plant in any area suffering from this destructive pest.

If you suffer from cats digging in your vegetable patch, try planting catnip in your borders or some pots away from your vegetables. This should distract the cats and stop them from bothering your plants.

Chervil (Anthriscus cerefolium)
Chervil is a popular herb in some countries, with leaves that have the taste of licorice, anise, parsley, and tarragon. It is a very interesting herb, and the flowers are also edible. The plant will typically grow between one and two feet tall, so be careful it doesn't shade out your other plants.

Chervil is a great companion for broccoli, radishes, and carrots. When grown near radishes, it makes the radishes crisper and hotter. When grown near lettuces, it will protect them from aphids. It also makes for an excellent companion for coriander (cilantro) and dill, with all three working well together in a container.

Be aware that chervil itself is very susceptible to aphids, making it a good trap crop. It is also popular with slugs, rabbits, and groundhogs.

Coriander / Cilantro (Coriandrum sativum)

Coriander, or cilantro as it is known in America, is a very popular culinary herb. The leaves are often referred to just as cilantro but the seeds, which are much spicier, are often referred to as coriander seeds. The fresh leaves are great to add a bit of spice to a salad or used in a wide variety of dishes. It's commonly used as a garnish and as frequently used in Indian cuisine.

Planting coriander near to spinach, chervil, tomatoes, and asparagus will benefit all of the plants, but planting beans or peas with coriander will help the growth of your coriander plant. Avoid planting this herb with fennel, which really does not like being planted with anything else.

Anise will help coriander plants grow strong and healthy while the coriander will help anise seeds to germinate faster.

One big benefit of coriander is that it will attract a wide variety of beneficial insects into your garden, including parasitic wasps and hoverflies. It will repel a variety of harmful insects, including spider mites, potato beetles, and aphids. An infusion of coriander leaves makes a spray that will kill spider mites. If you want maximum benefit from your coriander plants, choose a variety that bolts quickly, meaning it will produce flowers rapidly and start attracting the insects you want to your garden. Gardeners often sow seeds every few weeks to have the plant flowering throughout the year.

Dill (Anethum graveolens)

This wonderful herb is not as popular as it used to be, but fresh it brings out the flavor in a dish. Try it in your egg and potato salad for a great taste.

Dill is a very good companion plant, helping a wide variety of plants including all members of the brassica family except cabbage and cauliflower. It's also a good partner for other plants, including asparagus, chervil, cucumber, lettuce, onions, and sweet corn. Planting beans near dill helps the growth of the dill plants.

Although dill grows well with a lot of plants, there is a number you should avoid planting it near, including angelica, caraway, carrots, chili, peppers, aubergine (eggplant), fennel, potatoes, and lavender. Dill, carrots, and fennel are all members of the same family, meaning they can cross pollinate. If you want to avoid this, then be careful about how close you put these three plants.

When it is young, dill makes for an excellent companion for tomatoes, helping them to grow stronger and be healthier. However, as dill matures, it will stunt the growth of your tomatoes and attract tomato horn worms. Therefore if these two plants are grown together, either remove or harvest the dill before it matures to prevent damage to your tomato plants.

When it flowers, dill will attract beneficial insects such as parasitic wasps, hoverflies, and bees. It is also very popular with the swallowtail butterfly, its caterpillars feasting on dill.

Dill repels many harmful insects, including aphids, squash bugs, spider mites, and cabbage looper.

Fennel (Foeniculum vulgare)

Fennel is a very anti-social plant and makes for a poor companion for most other plants. Usually, fennel is located away from other plants because of this. The main benefit of fennel, apart from its culinary uses, is that it attracts beneficial insects such as bees, ladybugs, parasitic wasps, syrphid flies, and hoverflies.

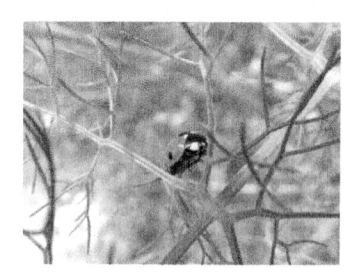

In the kitchen, fennel is great in Italian dishes, gives a curry additional sweetness and is a great flavor for sausages, any tomato based dishes, and soups. It has a strong taste and aroma, meaning it can deter some harmful insects from your vegetable garden.

The only companion plant for fennel is dill, but as these two cross-pollinate, it isn't an ideal pairing.

There are two other benefits from growing fennel. Fennel repels aphids as they find it extremely offensive. This herb is also a very good flea repellent. Old time gardeners would often say "plant fennel near your kennel" because of its ability to deter fleas. If you do own a kennel, put dried fennel leaves inside it to help keep fleas away from your dog.

Lemon Balm (Melissa officinalis)

Lemon balm is a wonderful herb, believed in medieval times to have almost miracle healing properties. As a member of the mint family, lemon balm grows by putting out rhizomes and will grow rampantly if planted directly in the soil. Like mint, lemon balm is best planted in containers and moved around your garden as required.

One of the major benefits of this plant is that it attracts beneficial and pollinating insects. It has a strong citrus aroma which many pests, including mosquitoes and gnats, find offensive.

Lemon balm can be planted with pretty much any plant. If grown in containers then you do not even need to worry about soil conditions. I find it is handy to bring into the greenhouse when I want to attract pollinators to my tomato and pepper plants.

Some of the best companions for lemon balm include tomatoes, squashes, melons, all brassicas, apples, basil, kiwi fruit, onions, and sage.

If you want to deter pests, then combine lemon balm with asters, daisies, geraniums, dill, marigolds, nasturtiums, lavender, parsley, chives, or mint. A combination of these plants will put off a lot of potential insect pests that will bother your plants.

Lovage (Levisticum officinale)

Lovage is a good herb to have in your garden. For the cook, lovage pairs well with potatoes and the seeds are delicious on bread. Its leaves make for a great flavoring for both soups and stews.

It can be planted in your garden as a companion for most plants. It helps improve the flavor and general health of many other plants. It is known as a particularly good companion for asparagus, which benefits from lovage being planted in the same bed.

Marjoram (Origanum majorana)

Marjoram is a positive delight to have in your garden. It is one of the best herbs to attract pollinating insects. When it flowers in the summer, it will be covered with bees, and the resulting honey is delicious!

In the kitchen, marjoram is great in just about any dish, whether meat, fish, or vegetable, so long as the dish isn't sweet. It is best added towards the end of cooking to retain the maximum amount of flavor.

Marjoram is a perennial, but is relatively tender, meaning most people treat it as an annual. However, I've overwintered it in the ground on my vegetable plot in the north of England, and it has done fine.

Marjoram makes for a good companion for most plants, helping to stimulate the growth of its neighbors. You can either plant this directly into the soil or in containers and move the containers around as required.

A good companion for marjoram is the stinging nettle, which improves the essential oil component of marjoram. However, you do have to contend with the stinging nettles trying to take over your garden. Saying that stinging nettles do make an excellent liquid compost!

As marjoram likes a well-draining, rich soil, it's best companions are those that like similar soil conditions, such as potatoes, radishes, onions, peas, corn, celery, and aubergine (eggplant).

Mint (Mentha)

Mint is a popular herb in the garden and comes in many different varieties including apple mint, peppermint, spearmint, and pineapple mint. Most of these variations benefit from the same companion planting as mint itself. All varieties are rampant and grow from shoots under the ground. They are best grown in pots where they can be moved around your plot.

It is a lovely herb to use in the kitchen, being great with boiled new potatoes (try using apple mint with potatoes for an amazing flavor). It is a popular herb in Middle Eastern cooking and is good as a mint sauce with roast lamb.

Mint is an excellent companion for a wide variety of plants, including beetroot, brassicas, pepper plants, aubergine (eggplant), kohlrabi, lettuce, and squashes. When planted near tomatoes, cabbage or peas, mint helps improve both their flavor and health. Broccoli and Brussels sprouts help mint to grow more vigorously.

Avoid planting mint near parsley and chamomile as they do not make good companions.

One property of mint is that its smell deters a wide range of insects. It is a common component of commercial insecticidal soaps. It can help repel ants, aphids, earwigs, slugs, snails, and spider mites. It is used as a component of insecticide sprays, but be careful not to get it on any flowers as you will deter pollinators.

One common claim with mint is that it repels mice, which hate the smell of it. Mint should be planted (or dried mint scattered) near any crops that suffer from mouse damage.

Oregano (Origanum vulgare)
Oregano is a popular culinary herb, frequently used in Italian and Greek cooking. It is good in any tomato dish and works well with both lamb and potatoes.

As a companion plant, oregano is a good companion for almost any vegetable plant. It can be dotted around your garden to help improve the health and flavor of your main crops. It has no known bad companions.

Oregano works particularly well with cucumber, cabbage, and cauliflower and helps to repel many different pests.

Parsley (Petroselinum crispum)
Another herb often used in cooking, parsley is great as a garnish and used in a wide variety of dishes, particularly soups, salads, and sauces. It is very commonly grown, and there are a few different varieties such as flat leaf and curly leaf, which have slightly different flavors.

Parsley is a good companion for many different plants including chives, corn, peppers, carrots, peas, onions, and tomatoes. It is a particularly good companion for asparagus, which grows much better when parsley is planted in the same bed. Avoid planting parsley with lettuce or mint as they do not grow well together.

For anyone who grows roses, parsley should be planted at the base of your rose plants to improve their fragrance. The flowers will smell much sweeter with parsley as a companion.

Parsley does attract insects to your garden. It is particularly attractive to the swallowtail butterfly, which lays its eggs on the leaves. The resulting caterpillars love parsley. When allowed to go to seed, parsley attracts hoverflies which will eat aphids and thrips, amongst other pests. Parsley also helps to repel harmful beetles.

Rosemary (Rosmarinus officinalis)

A lovely, perennial plant, rosemary is popular in both the kitchen and the garden. As a herb, it is delicious in bread and works well with a wide variety of dishes including poultry, lamb and any tomato dishes.

Rosemary tends to grow leggy when planted in the ground, needing pruning every year. It can successfully be grown in pots where it will typically retain a more compact shape.

As a companion, rosemary works well when planted with broccoli. The two together grow healthier and have a better flavor.

Rosemary is also a good companion for beans, cabbage, and peppers. It does not make a good companion for potatoes, pumpkins, or carrots. You will hear of carrots being a good pairing with rosemary. Although they should not be planted together, rosemary cuttings can be placed near to a crop of carrots to repel carrot fly.

Rosemary acts as a good deterrent for many harmful insects, including the cabbage moth, cabbage fly, bean beetle, and carrot fly.

Sage (Salvia officinalis)

Sage is less commonly grown in the garden but is great in stuffing, cheese dishes and salads. Added to dishes, it helps reduce the amount of salt required, making it a good herb for anyone on a low sodium diet.

It is known to deter both the carrot fly and cabbage moth due to its aroma. It benefits from being planted near both carrots and cabbages because of this. It is also a good companion for rosemary. Avoid planting sage near cucumbers as the two do not grow well together.

Summer Savory (Satureja hortensis)

Another herb that is less common in the garden, it is great in the kitchen. Summer savory works well with fish, chicken, and eggs as well as in soups and stews.

As a companion plant, summer savory is planted with onions and beans, where it improves their flavor and growth.

Tarragon (Artemisia dracunculus)

Tarragon is another herb that is not commonly found in the vegetable garden. It makes for a good companion for most vegetables and it great in the kitchen, particularly with fish or in salad dressings. This herb is commonly used in French cuisine.

Be careful when buying seeds for tarragon as many seeds are a variety known as Tagetes lucida, which is a substitute for tarragon and has a weaker flavor.

This plant is a great companion for eggplant (aubergine), though works well with virtually any vegetable plant. It is known as a 'nurse' plant, meaning it helps the growth and improves the flavor of anything it is grown with.

Thyme (Thymus vulgaris)
Thyme is another plant that comes in several different varieties. It is good in the kitchen, particularly with stews, casseroles, and tomato dishes. It is also a very good plant to grow if you are a beekeeper. It attracts a lot of pollinating insects, and the resulting honey is particularly special.

Plant thyme with cabbages as it deters the cabbage worm. It is also a good companion for strawberries and potatoes. Although lavender is often stated to be a good companion to thyme, there does not appear to be any significant benefits from the pairing. It looks like the two of them together attracts a lot of bees and works because they both like the same soil conditions.

Thyme will repel several different pests, including corn earworms, tomato hornworms, flea beetles, and cabbage worms. It attracts both pollinating and predatory insects.

Companion Planting With Trees

Companion planting is often used with vegetables, herbs, and flowers, but it is less commonly associated with trees. When the right types of plants are located with the right trees, there can be significant benefits for your trees and an increase in yield. In this chapter, you will learn about some of the good companions for trees which could help you make the most of your growing space.

Before you start, though, there are three trees that don't grow well with virtually anything else. White pine, hawthorn, and black walnut all prefer to grow by themselves. Black walnut exudes a chemical from its roots which kill plants growing near it. You will rarely see anything growing underneath one of these trees. If you are planting any of these three trees, then be aware you may not be able to grow anything else under their canopies.

The following plants are often grown with trees, making for good companion plants:

- Daffodils – an early season flower, these usually bloom not long before the tree does. This means that pollinating insects are already in the neighborhood of your trees and will be ready to pollinate their flowers for a good crop. Plant daffodils a minimum of six inches from the tree trunk in a circle around your tree.

- Chives – as a member of the onion (Allium) family, chives repel many different insects. However, when it flowers, it becomes irresistible to pollinating insects. Planted near your trees, this herb will help ensure your trees get pollinated.
- Bee Balm – this is another plant which attracts beneficial insects and pollinators to your trees. It tends to grow quite tall, but there are dwarf varieties available.
- Dill – another great companion due to the sheer volume of beneficial insects it attracts.
- Echinacea – as well as attracting beneficial insects, Echinacea works well under trees because it is drought tolerant. It has a deep tap root and brings up nutrients that are made available to your trees.
- Lupin – best known as a green manure, lupins fix nitrogen into the soil. As most fruit trees benefit from high levels of nitrogen, this flower is a great companion that can be dug into the soil over winter to increase nitrogen levels.

Most plants that flower and attract pollinating insects are beneficial to fruit trees. In most orchards, you will see plenty of flowers which bloom over several months, attracting beneficial insects into the garden. Planting many vegetables under fruit trees does not work because the trees use most of the water and nutrients, leaving little for the vegetables. The shade from the trees can also stunt the growth of many vegetables.

Apple Tree Companions

Apples are one of the most common trees grown in the vegetable garden. Most people grow apples on dwarf root stock and train their apples either as stepover apples or grown on espaliers. Growing in this manner allows better use of space as the trees either cast very little shade or the shade they do cast can be controlled. This allows you to plant vegetables and other useful crops with your apple trees. When grown in stepover form, your apple trees can form a productive, living hedge for your vegetable garden.

Many of the plants detailed above are good companions for apple trees as they attract beneficial, pollinating insects. Living mulches, such as chamomile, help to retain moisture and can be cut back regularly to add nutrients to the soil. Other plants, like Echinacea that have long tap roots, are useful companions to pull nutrients up from deeper in the soil.

Comfrey is another good company, though be aware it is very invasive and hard to dig out. The leaves make for an excellent fertilizer when mixed with water and left to rot. Nasturtiums are good to plant with apple trees as a trap crop because they attract aphids.

As a companion, chives will help to prevent apple scab and also keep away rabbits and deer. Planting dogwood will attract predatory insects that will eat many common apple tree pests. Many of the plants we have discussed earlier are useful companions for apple trees for their pest repelling abilities.

Companion planting works well for trees, but you need to be careful that whatever you plant will grow successfully under the trees. Planting the right plants can help you avoid some of the common problems trees suffer from and help attract pollinating insects to ensure a good crop.

Companion Planting for Pest Control

As you have learned from the many different types of companion plant, they are great for keeping pests down. For the home gardener, pests are one of the biggest problems that can destroy your crops. Although there are many chemical sprays you could use, a lot of people prefer to avoid chemicals where possible. We won't get into the organic vs. non-organic debate here, it is your decision, but companion planting can help reduce your need for chemicals and keep pests under control naturally.

Companion planting is a case of learning what works in your area. Different plants work together in different types of soil and locations. Companion plants can be extremely good at deterring pests, but you must remember that some of them take time to build up that protection. Chives will protect against apple scab, but it can take up to three years before they provide full protection.

You also need to remember that once an infestation has occurred, companion planting may not provide a complete solution because there are too many pests. Planting onions next to your cabbages to protect against cabbage moth will work if the onions are planted first, but planting the onions after the moths have taken up residence will not provide as many benefits.

There will be some years where pest infestations are much more serious. Pest populations fluctuate, with them being lower in some years and in others being at positive plague levels. Again, in high population years, companion planting will provide some assistance but may not provide a complete solution.

It also depends on what people are growing near your vegetable plot. If your neighbors have kindly grown lots of plants that attract pests, then you may find higher than normal populations in your vegetable garden, which the companion plants may not fully protect against. Alternatively, your neighbors may be growing plants which attract beneficial insects, which is obviously very helpful.

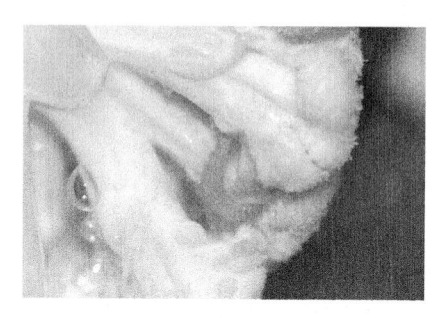

Companion planting provides help combating pests and is used in combination with other methods. You remain vigilant and act against any pest infestations, removing them by hand before they can get established or using organic or non-organic pest controls where necessary.

While some companion plants will deter pests, which we have discussed earlier, others are in place to attract beneficial insects which feed on pests. You can help attract more of these helpful insects by providing them with homes and an environment where they can thrive. Some of the beneficial insects you want to attract into your garden include:

- Parasitoid wasps which feed on grubs, caterpillars, and aphids
- Lacewing larvae which feed on aphids
- Ground beetles which feed on a variety of ground-based pests
- Hover flies which feed on many different insects, including caterpillars and leafhoppers
- Ladybug larvae which feed on aphids
- Robber flies which feed on insects such as leafhoppers and caterpillars

One of the keys to successful pest control with companion planting is diverse planting. Covering your vegetable plot with onions in the hope that it will control all pests probably won't work. You will need a variety of plants, even a variety of companion plants that attract the same types of insects for it to be truly effective.

As well as this, the plants need to be effective at attracting beneficial insects throughout the growing season. If your companion plants flower in June and start to die back at the end of the month, they are not going to provide any protection from July onwards. Succession planting can help, but diversity will ensure the companion plants are effective through the whole of the growing season.

A Robber Fly

This is one of the most common mistakes people make when companion planting, so please ensure that your chosen companion plants are flowering and able to attract beneficial insects for the whole time your vegetable crop is at risk. If not, those insects that you are trying to attract will go elsewhere when you need them the most.

Although beneficial insects will eat pests, there are times in their lifecycle when they do not. At these times, they need somewhere to live and food such as nectar or pollen. Providing the essentials for all stages of the beneficial insect's lifespan means that they take up residence in your vegetable garden and provides greater protection for a longer period. A hedgerow or pile of fallen logs can provide an excellent home. Early season flowers can provide much-needed nourishment for their young, keeping these insects near your vegetable plot.

If you want a hedgerow but are concerned about the lack of productivity of one, grow a hedgerow of fruit trees. Either use dwarf or patio varieties or train your plants to grow in stepover or espalier forms along wires.

What Do Beneficial Insects Need?
So, what is it that these beneficial insects require to make a home in your vegetable plot and work to keep pest populations down?

- Ground cover – low growing plants such as mint, rosemary or thyme provide cover for all sorts of ground beetles. Hiding in these

plants provides them with protection from predators so they can live out their lives hunting pests for you.
- Shade – a shady, protected area is important for laying eggs. Some people will have a wild or slightly wild area of their garden specifically for beneficial insects.
- Tiny flowers – many of the predatory wasps are very small and need small flowers to attract them such as any member of the Umbelliferae family, e.g. Fennel, dill, coriander, clovers, yarrow and so on.
- Composite flowers – larger flowers such as chamomile and daisy are great for attracting robber flies, predatory wasps and hover flies. Any member of the mint family also helps.

We'll talk more about attracting beneficial insects in a little while.

Herbs to Deter Pests

Herbs are particularly good companion plants. Not only do you get the benefit of them repelling pests, but you can also use them in the kitchen, either fresh or dried.

Many of these herbs look great, have pretty flowers, and have a lovely fragrance. They work together with other factors, including the environment to provide protection. Try the different companion plants and see what effect they have as it does vary from place to place. Some of these companion plants exude chemicals that can take months or even a year to build up enough to deter pests.

Here are some of the more commonly found pests and companion plants that traditionally repel them.

- Ants – catnip, mints (including peppermint and spearmint), tansy, and wormwood
- Aphids – catnip, chives, coriander (cilantro), chrysanthemum (dried and crushed), eucalyptus, fennel, feverfew (best planted near roses to attract aphids), garlic, marigold, mint, mustard, nasturtium, onion, and oregano

- Asparagus Beetle – basil, pot marigold (Calendula), nasturtium, parsley, tansy, and tomato
- Bean Beetle – marigold, nasturtium, rosemary, and summer savory
- Black Flea Beetle – sage
- Cabbage Looper – dill, eucalyptus, garlic, hyssop, peppermint/spearmint, nasturtium, onion, sage, thyme, and wormwood
- Cabbage Maggot – garlic, marigold, radishes, sage, and wormwood
- Cabbage Moth – hyssop, mint, oregano, rosemary, sage, summer savory, tansy, and thyme
- Cabbage Worm – celery, thyme, and tomatoes
- Carrot Fly – alliums (onion family), lettuce, rosemary, sage, tobacco (be aware this can be illegal to grow in some areas), and wormwood
- Colorado Potato Beetle – catnip, coriander (cilantro), eucalyptus, marigold, nasturtium, onions, and tansy
- Corn Earworm – cosmos, geranium, and marigold
- Cucumber Beetle – catnip, marigold, nasturtium, radishes, and tansy
- Flea Beetle – catnip (steeped in water and used as a spray), garlic, mint, ruse, sage, tansy, tobacco, and wormwood
- Flies – basil, ruse, and tansy
- Japanese Beetle – catnip, chives, garlic, hydrangea, pansy, rue, and tansy
- Leafhopper – chrysanthemum (dried and crushed), geranium, and petunias
- Mexican Bean Beetle – marigold, petunias, rosemary, and summer savory
- Mice – tansy, and wormwood
- Mosquitoes – basics, garlic, geranium, and rosemary
- Moths – lavender, rosemary, and wormwood
- Peach Borer – garlic
- Nematodes – marigolds (takes about a year for the chemicals to

build up in the soil, pot marigolds
- Onion Fly – garlic
- Slugs & Snails – fennel, garlic, rosemary, and sage
- Spider Mites – coriander (cilantro)
- Squash Bugs – catnip, mint, nasturtiums, petunias, radishes, and tansy
- Squash Vine Borer – radishes
- Striped Cucumber Beetle – tansy
- Striped Pumpkin Beetle – nasturtiums
- Ticks – garlic, and lavender
- Tomato Hornworms – borage, calendula (pot marigold), dill, marigold, and petunias
- White Cabbage Moth – mint
- Whitefly – basil, marigold, oregano, peppermint, and thyme

As you can see, there are a lot of different ways of protecting your plants from pests. Try to choose companion plants to provide protection throughout the growing season. These will help deter pests, but keep a close eye on your plants anyway as some pests may slip through your defenses.

Allelopathy Explained

Allelopathy is best described as chemical warfare between plants. It's the ability of one plant to suppress another and to take advantage of that situation. The word is derived from two Ancient Greek words, 'allelon' meaning each other and 'pathos' which means to suffer.

Therefore, allelopathic plants deliberately create adverse growing conditions which stunts and kills off neighboring plants. This can be by reducing germination rates or seedling growth or just plain killing off competing plants. Used wisely, allelopathic plants can be a great alternative to chemicals!

Plants compete for resources such as space, water, nutrition, and sunlight. Some compete by growing rapidly, others spread out wide or send down deep roots. Other plants have developed chemical tools for getting the resources they require to flourish.

Allelopathic plants release compounds from the roots into the soil which then suppress or kill their neighbors as they are sucked up through their root systems. These harmful chemicals are, unsurprisingly, known as allelochemicals. Some of these chemicals can go as far as changing the level of chlorophyll production which can then slow down or even stop photosynthesis, which obviously leads to the death of the plant.

A lot of allelopathic plants release chemicals in gas form from small pores in their leaves. As their neighbors absorb these gasses, they are either suppressed or killed.

Some allelopathic plants deal with the competition when their leaves fall to the ground. The leaves decompose and release chemicals which then inhibit nearby plants.

There are a lot of different plants that have allelopathic tendencies, but it isn't particularly common. Sometimes, however, you can very easily plant an allelopathic plant near one of its victims without realizing it and wonder why some of your plants struggle to grow.

The black walnut tree is probably the master of chemical warfare in the plant kingdom. Its leaves, roots, nut hulls and buds have allelopathic properties, and it also secretes juglone into the soil, which inhibits respiration in many plants. In fact, the black walnut guards its resources so jealously, that virtually nothing will grow near to one. Many a gardener has rejoiced at the black walnut tree in their garden until their realized that nothing will grow near it.

Allelopathic characteristics can be found in any part of a plant, whether it is the root, bark, flowers, seeds, fruits, leaves, or pollen. It varies from plant to plant, though the majority of plants store their allelopathic chemicals in their leaves.

Some common plants that are known to have allelopathic properties include:

- English laurel (Prunus laurocerasus)
- Elderberry (Sambucus)
- Bearberry (Arctostaphylos uva-Uris)
- Rhododendron
- Junipers, which hamper the growth of grasses
- Perennial rye hampers the growth of apple trees
- Sugar maple hampers the growth of yellow birch and white spruce

If you think about where you see these plants growing, you will see very little growing underneath or near them.

There is a lot of research underway into allelopathic plants, and the list of plants is regularly being updated. These plants are very interesting to farmers for their properties, which could well find their way into genetically modified seeds.

The advantage of allelochemicals is that they can produce natural herbicides and pesticides. Planting the right plants together as companions will keep down certain weeds, which can reduce reliance on chemical herbicides. When pairings are chosen well, the allelopathic plant will even have a positive effect on your chosen vegetable crop.

Allelopathic research is still very much in its infancy as researchers try to understand this interaction between plants. There are some research papers published, and you can use this effect to your benefit in your garden. If you have established plants already present in your garden and are struggling to grow anything else, it may be that one of these plants has allelopathic properties.

Be aware that allelochemicals can build up in the soil and it can take several years for the levels of these chemicals to drop so that other plants will grow. Years ago, I removed an English laurel tree from my garden as it was too large. Underneath was bare soil, nothing had grown there but when I dug over the soil and added manure, everything I planted died. It was several years and a lot of fertilizer and compost before anything would grow in that area again. If you have to remove allelopathic plants, then you may want to consider removing 12-18 inches of soil and replacing it if you struggle to get anything to grow in that space.

Attracting Beneficial Insects

We talked earlier about how companion planting can help you combat the many pests in your garden. This did touch on attracting beneficial insects, but in this chapter, you are going to learn more about what beneficial insects are and how to bring them into your garden.

The benefit of these insects is that they prey on many of the pests that will devour your crops. Some people build small ponds to attract frogs and toads, which then eat slugs, which is great. As you are about to learn, you can grow certain plants and create an environment that is attractive to insects which will help you in the garden.

Which Insects Are Beneficial

There are literally millions of types of insect, but not all of them are pests determined to devour your crops. There are a lot of species which are referred to under the umbrella term of 'beneficial insects' which provide a natural form of pest control. For many gardeners, including myself, they are an essential part of organic and natural gardening.

There are many reasons to attract beneficial insects, including:

- Reducing your reliance on chemical pesticides, which helps you to grow organically and saves you money.
- Chemical pesticides will kill pests, but they also decimate the beneficial insect population. In the long-term, this is bad news for your garden as you are wiping out the population of natural predators, so you end up becoming completely reliant on

chemicals. Pesticides do have their place and use, particularly during severe infestations, but they should be used sparingly and only when necessary.
- With the farming industry being so reliant on chemicals, more and more insects are developing resistance to these pesticides. If you can avoid using chemicals, then you are helping to prevent this resistance from developing and naturally controlling pests on your vegetable plot. To kill resistant pests requires stronger chemicals, which have a greater negative effect on beneficial insects and potentially your health too when ingested through your freshly grown produce.

In the majority of cases, you will naturally be attracting beneficial insects into your vegetable garden. By planting the right types of plants, these insects will flock to your plot where they will take up residence and feast on the destructive pests.

However, there are occasions when you may artificially introduce beneficial insects into your garden, in which case you need to think carefully.

Depending on the type of insect you are introducing, you may need to have a permit, even if importing insects from a different state. Certainly, you will if ordering insects from another country. Check the local regulations and rules to determine you can import these beneficial insects into your area.

If you have neighbors nearby, then talk to them and tell them what you are planning. If they use chemical sprays, then this could have a negative impact on your beneficial insects, and they may even be willing to share the cost and the benefits.

Providing an optimal living environment is important, particularly if you are buying in beneficial insects. Before they arrive, ensure that you have established an environment they can live in and that there are sufficient quantities of their prey in your garden for them to feed on. If this isn't present, then your insects will leave home looking for somewhere better to live or simply die off.

Here are some of the most commonly found beneficial insects with information about what they eat and the environment they prefer.

Ladybugs

These carnivorous insects feed on green and black aphids as well as red spider mites. Organic growers and gardeners love them, trying to attract these into their gardens. Every year ladybugs, or ladybirds as they are known in the UK, will lay hundreds of eggs. The larvae will eat thousands of aphids before maturing, hence the importance of providing a habitat for both this insect in both adult and larvae form. Typically, a ladybug will live for up to three years so long as it avoids being another predators lunch!

There are several plants that attract ladybugs, including:

- Tansy
- Fennel
- Dill
- Cinquefoil
- Yarrow
- Alyssum
- Penstemon

Ladybugs feed on some common garden pests, including:

- Aphids
- Colorado potato beetles
- Fleas
- Mites
- Whitefly

Spiders
A surprising number of people don't like spiders, which is understandable as they aren't my favorite critter either. However, they are very useful in the garden as they eat a lot of different pests. Spiders will naturally find a home in your garden, but you can attract more to your vegetable plot.

Spiders can be attracted to your garden with a number of plants and environments. Taller plants attract web weaving spiders which will catch more flying insects, some aphids, and grasshoppers. Predatory spiders like somewhere dark to hide and enjoy mulches for that reason. They will hunt many different pests including caterpillars, grasshoppers, and aphids.

Ground Beetles
These are your best friend as they are very voracious predators. These will eat almost anything, but are particularly fond of slugs and snails! Their

eating habits will mean they won't get invited to the dinner table; they vomit on their prey, and the digestive enzymes start to dissolve their food.

Ground beetles are often killed by beer traps put down for slugs, as they walk along and fall in. Make sure there is a lip on your beer trap which will prevent these beneficial predators from drowning in the beer.

Most ground beetles are nocturnal and need somewhere shady to hide during the day. A pile of stones or logs or some leaf litter will give them a good place to hide out during the day.

Ground beetles are attracted to your garden by several plants, including:

- Clover
- Amaranthus
- Evening Primrose

The ground beetle will dine on many different pests, including:

- Slugs and snails
- Cutworms
- Colorado potato beetles
- Caterpillars

These are definitely worth protecting and looking after in your garden because they will help to keep the pest levels down naturally.

Parasitic (Braconid) Wasps

These are very different from the wasps that bother a lot of gardeners. They tend to be smaller and will not sting you, unlike their bigger and more vicious cousins.

The lifecycle of these wasps is considered a little gruesome, but they benefit your garden in helping to control pest levels. This wasp will lay its egg in host insects. Once the egg has hatched, the larvae eat the host alive and then emerge as an adult. This family of wasps hunts many different pests including caterpillars, ants, aphids, and sawflies.

Parasitic wasps can be purchased and introduced to your garden. Just be aware of any local regulations that may affect their introduction and tell your neighbors what you are doing so they don't accidentally kill off your new garden helpers.

A wide variety of plants attracts parasitic wasps, including:

- Yarrow
- Dill
- Parsley
- Lemon Balm
- Lobelia
- Marigold
- Cosmos
- Alyssum
- Cinquefoil

They prey on a lot of different destructive insects, including:

- Aphids
- Caterpillars
- Tomato hornworm
- Tobacco hornworm

Damsel Bugs
Another great insect to attract into your garden, these are not fussy eaters and will prey on pretty much any insect that causes problems in your garden. In Europe, they live in orchards where they eat gypsy moths and red spider mites. This insect will overwinter in vegetation and appreciates somewhere to hide out between meals.

Although damsel bugs can bite, their bite isn't poisonous and tends to have no effect other than a minor irritation to the victim. They can occasionally eat leaves, but not usually to the extent that causes crop damage. Providing there is sufficient prey for them, they are unlikely to touch your vegetable crop.

Damsel bugs are attracted to your garden by plants including:

- Alfalfa,
- Fennel
- Caraway
- Spearmint

They eat lots of common garden pests, including:

- Aphids
- Cabbage worms
- Caterpillars
- Corn earworms
- Leafhoppers
- Potato beetles
- Spider mites

By growing some ground cover and low hanging plants, you can attract damsel bugs into your garden where they can help control pests.

Green Lacewings
These are particularly attractive insects that are common in British gardens. With their delicate, lacy wings you could be forgiven for thinking these innocent little creatures are of no use in your garden.

Don't be fooled by their good looks! These are voracious predators in both adult and larvae forms and will eat vast amounts of insect eggs and aphids. The larvae have large jaws which interlock to make pincers on which their prey is impaled. The larvae are very good at clearing your garden of soft-bodied pests.

Lacewings are attracted into your garden by several different plants, including:

- Angelica
- Coriander
- Cosmos
- Dandelion
- Dill
- Fennel
- Yarrow

Some of the insects eaten by lacewings include:

- Aphids
- Caterpillars
- Leafhoppers
- Mealybugs
- Whitefly

Soldier Beetles
Both adults and larvae are useful in pest control. The female lays her eggs in the soil where they overwinter, pupating in the spring. Therefore, you need to leave some areas of soil undisturbed overwinter so these eggs can mature.

Soldier beetles also eat pollen, so pollen-bearing plants can help to attract them into your garden. Other plants that attract them include:

- Goldenrod

- Marigold
- Milkweed
- Wild lettuce
- Zinnia

These beneficial insects prey on many different insects, including:

- Aphids
- Caterpillars
- Corn rootworms
- Cucumber beetles
- Grasshopper eggs

These are an interesting insect to look at and will help keep pests under control.

Tachinid Flies
Adult tachinid flies closely resemble the typical housefly and so are often mistaken for them. These are a parasitic insect and lays its eggs in host insects. Depending on the species of fly, either eggs or live young are placed inside a host insect where they then eat their way out. Some species will even lay eggs on plants where host insects live which then hatch and eat them.

These insects love flowering plants such as anything in the dill or aster family. You may see caterpillars on your plants with white eggs on their backs. Tachinid flies have attacked these and the eggs will soon hatch and bury their way into their host.

Tachinid flies can be bought, or you can attract them into your garden with a variety of plants including:

- Aster
- Buckwheat
- Carrots
- Cilantro (coriander)
- Chamomile
- Dill
- Fennel
- Feverfew
- Parsley

- Ox-eye and Shasta daisies

They prey on a lot of different pests, including:

- Caterpillars
- Colorado potato beetles
- Corn earworms
- Cutworms
- Earwigs
- Gypsy moths
- Japanese beetles
- Mexican bean beetles
- Sawfly beetles
- Squash bugs

Hoverflies

These are frequently confused with wasps as they share a black and yellow coloring, but they do not sting. They also hover (which wasps do not), do not have long antennae and are typically smaller than stinging wasps. There are lots of different species of hoverfly, and they can fly as fast as 40km/h in short bursts.

The adult hoverfly will feed on pollen and nectar, so it is the larvae you are particularly interested in. They are voracious predators and feed on a wide variety of garden pests, including aphids. These helpful insects not only assist with pollination, but their young keeps the pest population down too.

Hoverflies will naturally find their way into your garden, but you can attract more of them with plants such as:

- Alyssum
- Cosmos
- Dill
- Lemon balm
- Mallow
- Marigold
- Yarrow

Hoverfly larvae prey on some garden pests including:

- Aphids
- Caterpillars
- Scale insects

Predatory Mites

Humid environments attract these mites such as polytunnels (hoop houses) and greenhouses, where they are most welcome as they prey on spider mites! Spider mites can be a serious problem in greenhouses and very hard to control.

Predatory mites can find their way into your greenhouse, but more often people will buy these beneficial insects and introduce them to the environment.

When there are no spider mites for them to feed on, they will feed on pollen from your plants, helping with pollination.

Solitary Bees

There are lots of species of solitary bee, which does not live in colonies, choosing to live by itself instead. In Britain alone, there are over 200 different species of solitary bee, including the masonry bee, which is often mistaken for a hornet or wasp.

These bees can look like wasps or honeybees, but they are no threat whatsoever to you. The females dig nests, which are then stocked with food (nectar and pollen) and sealed. The young are left to fend for themselves. These bees will usually nest under the ground, often being found under sheds, in piles or logs and so on. You can help encourage them to your garden by making an insect hotel.

These are vital pollinators and should be encouraged into your garden with flowering plants such as:

- Catnip
- Fuchsia
- Heather
- Lavender
- Marjoram
- Viburnum

You now know about some of the beneficial insects that you want to attract into your garden. Of course, there are many more insects, and some will depend on where in the world you live. In some area praying mantis is a beneficial insect, but here in England, I won't ever see one in the wild.

Growing the right types of plants will help attract these insects into your garden and should be part of any gardener's plan. Chemicals should be avoided where possible because they indiscriminately kill both beneficial and harmful insects. With certain chemicals, the residue will persist for the rest of the growing season, which can prevent beneficial insects from returning.

Building Homes and Nests

Flowers will help attract beneficial insects onto your vegetable plot. However, it is the larvae of many of these insects that provide the benefits, so it is in your best interests to encourage the insects to take up residence somewhere in your vegetable garden.

Providing a habitat where beneficial insects can not only live but survive overwinter is going to help keep these insects on your plot so that the larvae can do their work and feast on the pests eating your plants.

Different insects have different requirements. Some just want ground cover to hide under, some need to lay their eggs in the soil which is undisturbed over winter, and others need more elaborate accommodation.

One of the most popular ways of providing a home to beneficial insects is to make or buy an insect hotel. These can be bought in a variety of sizes and shapes. If you don't want to make one, then the store bought bug hotels are ideal because they will give beneficial insects a home and help increase their populations within your vegetable garden.

If you want to make your own, then it is easy enough and can be done at virtually no cost. Remember, these insects aren't expecting a five star Hilton hotel. Their criteria for a hotel pretty much ends at dry, out of the wind and away from predators!

Most home-made insect hotels are made from reclaimed materials. Anything you can lay your hands on will do. The simplest type of hotel is a wooden box, open at one end, stuffed with sticks, bamboo, plastic drink bottles, bits of pipe and anything else that an insect can crawl into and build a nest. If you want to go all out, use some tiles, felting or other roofing material to make it watertight.

Think about the type of materials your beneficial insects will want to settle down in, and fill your bug hotel with them. Your hotel doesn't have to be all one material for one type of interest. The best ones are a combination of different materials which provide a home for a number of different insects,

Materials you can consider using include:

- Drilled wood – solitary bees and some predatory wasps will be attracted to wood with holes drilled in it. So long as the holes are big enough for the insects, they will crawl in and lay their eggs. Drill holes in a variety of sizes from 5mm (0.2") to 10mm (0.4") in diameter which will allow different species of bee to take up residence.
- Rotting logs – wood boring beetles will make their homes here, and their larvae will eat through the wood. This level should be at the bottom of your hotel, so the logs remain damp. Mix in some other plant matter which will decay, attracting woodlice, millipedes, and centipedes, the latter of which eat slugs. Spiders will also make their homes here.
- Twigs and sticks – bundle together sticks of different sizes to provide a home for ground beetles. Ladybugs will also take up residence, as will hoverflies.
- Bamboo canes – The hollow stems provide a great home for solitary bees who will lay their eggs in the bamboo and seal the hole up behind them.
- Straw or rolled up cardboard – this makes a great home for lacewings. Put it in an empty plastic bottle (cut one end off first) to prevent it getting soggy and unattractive as a home.

Bug hotels are a great idea to build and can be a fun project for children to be involved in. However, you need to put it somewhere that the insects can get to it.

It needs to be in a sheltered part of your vegetable garden, away from constant human traffic. It needs to be out of the prevailing wind too. Solitary bees like a sunny aspect whereas most other insects prefer damper conditions. To encourage beneficial insects to take up residence faster, place it near a hedge, pond, or flower garden.

As well as your bug hotel, you can attract beneficial insects by leaving a log pile in a little-used corner, creating a small pond (even a washing up bowl sunk into the ground will help) or sowing some wildflowers.

When you attract insects into your vegetable garden, they will not only help you combat the many pests that will devour your crops but also support other wildlife further up the food chain, which is equally important.

Other Beneficial Creatures

We have spent a lot of time talking about beneficial insects. However, there are several other animals that you also want to attract into your garden because they will help to keep pest populations under control.

Building a small wildlife pond in one corner of your plot will attract frogs into your vegetable garden. Sure, some people are a bit squeamish where they are concerned, but frogs are your friend. They feast on slugs plus the water in the pond becomes a water source for local wildlife, attracting a wide variety of birds and animals to your garden.

Encouraging native birds into your garden will help keep the insect population under control. A word of warning though, do not attract pigeons into your garden as they will quite happily eat your plants as well as any food you leave out for them! If you are feeding the birds, make sure that pigeons cannot land on or near the feeders and eat from them. The pigeons are a nuisance plus they will discourage smaller birds, which feed on insects, from visiting your garden. Always net your brassicas and peas if there are pigeons in your area as they will decimate these crops.

Flowers are a great addition to your garden as they will attract hummingbirds and even butterflies, though net any crops that the latter may decide to lay eggs on.

Attracting toads, lizards, and snakes into your garden is highly beneficial because they will also help keep the harmful pest population under control. Depending on the types of snakes in your area, they could also help keep the rodent population down and prevent a lot of damage. Mice are well known for digging up and eating seeds or chewing on ripe vegetables.

For anyone who lives in an area plagued by mosquitoes, bats are a very beneficial predator to attract because they feast on mosquitoes. Build a bat house, and they will come and help keep the mosquito population under some control.

Hedgehogs are another welcome visitor to a vegetable garden. These harmless creatures will amble around your garden happily eating all the slugs they can find, so are well worth attracting into your garden. Remember to leave a bowl of water out for them, particularly on hot summer days. They can also take up residence in your compost piles, so be very careful when turning these if there are hedgehogs in your garden.

Attracting these animals into your garden is a case of understanding which ones are in your local area and then building an environment that they will appreciate and settle down in. Try to make sure they have a safe haven throughout the year. If you are unsure what, beneficial animals live in your area, speak to your local wildlife officer who will be able to advise you.

Some people may let ducks, geese, or chickens loose in their garden to forage and keep slugs and snails at bay. The benefit of these is, of course, fresh eggs, but there is a downside too! These delightful fowl will quite happily not only eat your seedlings but also eat most of your crops too, but they will give you some great manure in return. I've known some people who have let their chickens run free in their vegetable garden to control the slug population and find their plants decimated by curious chickens. Net or raise up anything you want to protect to prevent the chickens from destroying it.

When attracting wild animals into your garden, avoid feeding them directly. Firstly, this can encourage them to get into trouble by approaching other humans who may not appreciate them as you do. Secondly, it can reduce their ability to survive on their own as they become dependent on you for food. Also, avoid the use of pesticides and herbicides in your garden as this can be very harmful to these beneficial animals and discourage them from giving you a helping hand.

The Importance of Crop Rotation

One subject that needs to be addressed is that of crop rotation. This is very important for the health of your plants and soil, being the principle of not growing the same crops in the same piece of ground year after year. If you do, then you are encouraging the build-up of harmful pests and diseases in the soil which can wreck your crops. Rotating your crops between plots means planting in fresh soil and that many potentially serious problems never get a chance to get established.

A big part of companion planting is to interplant one crop with another. For example, in crop rotation, you wouldn't grow garlic in the same bed two years in a row. However, with companion planting, you may plant the odd garlic bulb in between many of your other plants.

You may then think you can't grow garlic again in those areas, even as a companion plant. However, as you are only growing a small amount of garlic, you are very unlikely to suffer from a build-up of pathogens in the soil. Therefore, when companion planting individual or small amounts of plants, crop rotation can go out of the window. It is okay to plant companions in the same spots year after year, though if you do notice any consistent problems or suffer from any diseases, you will have to move them.

For anyone growing larger amounts of vegetables, crop rotation is very important. You need to move crops every year so that they are not always being grown in the same place. The average home gardener will have to practice crop rotation, though in smaller gardens it can be tricky. Always keep a written record of what you have planted where so that you can rotate your crops correctly. Anyone planting in rows, blocks or filling raised beds with one or two plants will need to practice crop rotation to reduce potential problems.

Some perennial crops such as strawberries, rhubarb and asparagus do not fit into any crop rotation plan. You are not going to dig up any of these and move them every year; you would never get a crop. These are planted in one place for their lifetime, with the soil being conditioned every year to keep it nutritious and healthy.

Some annual crops such as French and runner beans, sweet corn, and salad crops can be grown pretty much anywhere, though try to avoid growing them too often in the same place. Other crops like pumpkins, courgettes, squashes, potatoes, tomatoes, carrots, onions, and all members of the brassica family need to be rotated every year because pests and diseases can quickly build up in the soil.

Blight, for example, which affects tomatoes and potatoes can overwinter in the soil, particularly if diseased foliage is accidentally dug in or diseased potatoes are left in the ground, which always happens. Moving the plant the following year means this disease can die off and will not be able to immediately re-infect your crop.

Crop rotation is usually planned over winter before you start planting anything out. That gives you time to prepare the soil, if necessary, and mark out beds where necessary.

Crop rotation has a lot of benefits for you, the vegetable gardener, including:

- Improves soil fertility – rotating crops prevents one particular vegetable from exhausting the soil of nutrients. Done properly, it allows you to build up nutrient levels in the soil, such as planting beans and digging in the roots to fix nitrogen.
- Weed control – planting squashes and potatoes provides a lot of ground cover, which helps to suppress weeds and prevent the problems associated with them.
- Pest/disease control – as soil borne pests and diseases tend to target a specific family of plants, you can prevent this damage simply by not growing the same vegetable in the same place for three to four years. In this time, the pest or disease should have died off and won't be a problem when you re-introduce the original vegetable back to that bed. Crop rotation is used to avoid a variety

of diseases such as white rot in onions and club root in brassicas.

Rotating Your Crops
You can make crop rotation as simple or as complex as you want. I tend to keep it on the simple side because I find it much easier to keep track of. Your plants are grouped into five groups, excluding perennial plants such as rhubarb and asparagus.

1. Brassicas – Brussels sprouts, cabbage, cauliflower, kale, kohlrabi, oriental greens (including chards), radish, swede, and turnips (rutabaga)
2. Legumes – broad beans and peas (both French and runner beans have fewer problems with soil-borne diseases and can be planted anywhere)
3. Onions – garlic, leek, onion, and shallot
4. Potato family – potato, and tomato (although peppers and aubergines are in the same family, they have fewer problems and can be grown anywhere except when an area suffers from blight and then you will want to include them in your crop rotation scheme)
5. Root crops – beetroot, carrot, celeriac, celery, fennel (though this doesn't get on with most plants so is planted towards the edge of most vegetable gardens), parsley, parsnip, and any other root crop.

Each year you simply move each section of your vegetable garden one step forward, so the bed that contained legumes will have brassicas in the following year. Let me give you a very simple, three-year crop rotation plan based on the majority of crops being brassicas and potatoes:

First Year
- Bed One – Potatoes
- Bed Two – Legumes, onions, and root crops
- Bed Three – Brassicas

Second Year
- Bed One – Legumes, onions, and root crops
- Bed Two – Brassicas
- Bed Three – Potatoes

Year Three
- Bed One – Brassicas
- Bed Two – Potatoes

- Bed Three – Legumes, onions, and root crops

The same principles apply when performing a four-year crop rotation plan. Depending on the size of your vegetable garden you may work on either a three or four-year schedule. Smaller gardens work well on a three-year rotation plan, whereas larger gardens benefit from a four-year rotation plan.

In my crop rotation plan, I have one or two beds that are devoted to onions or shallots as I use a lot of them. I have another bed dedicated to garlic. These form part of my crop rotation plan. However, I also plant some onions near to my brassicas as part of my companion planting, and usually, some kohlrabi makes its way into my onion bed for the same reason. As the brassicas are rotated every year, so the onions are also rotated every year, keeping to the principles of crop rotation.

This works and is fine; you can do the same. However, if I were to see any evidence of white rot or other problems in the onions, I would avoid planting any onions, even as companion plants, in that bed for several years.

Crop rotation is an important tool in natural, organic gardening and will help minimize diseases and pests in your garden. A well thought out crop rotation plan nicely compliments your companion planting, helping to reduce your reliance on chemicals as you naturally control the pests on your vegetable plot.

BENEFICIAL WEEDS

As gardeners, weeds are the bane of our lives and we all hate them. They grow faster than our vegetables, even growing faster than we can pull them out of the soil and can quickly overwhelm you. Weed control is a very important part of gardening and mulches, weed membranes and hard work are the best ways to control them.

My strongest recommendation regarding weeds is to cover any area that you are not planting with a thick mulch of manure (three to four inches deep), tarps or heavy duty weed membrane. This will prevent the weeds growing back and help stop you getting overwhelmed. In winter, I will put a thick mulch of manure on my beds and then cover them with thick, black weed membrane. This then needs a quick dig over in the spring, and it is ready to plant in with minimal weeds under the covering.

However, some weeds are beneficial to your garden and will help your crops. We talked about green manures earlier in the book, some of which are often considered to be weeds, but as a green manure, they are invaluable.

Weeds, though, can do a lot to help you out including:

- Protecting soil – as weeds grow quickly, they can cover bare ground and protect it from washing away in the rain. Planting a green manure in these cases can give you the best of both worlds!
- Fertilizing the soil – a lot weeds accumulate nutrients from the soil into their leaves, so digging them into the soil and allowing them to rot will put the nutrients back into the soil. This is why green

manures work so well.

- Soil conditioner – as the leaves or roots break down in the soil, they will aerate it and condition it for you. Digging weeds into the soil is a key component in the no-dig garden philosophy.
- Attracting beneficial insects – weeds often live out their lives fairly quickly, flowering several times in a single growing season in some cases. The flowers can attract beneficial insects to your garden, and the ground cover provides shelter for other beneficial insects. However, left unchecked they can also provide nourishment and a home for a wide variety of pests. If dandelions get established on my plot I tend to leave them until they flower and the bees have feasted on them, then I remove the flower heads before they can seed.

There are a lot of different weeds you can use as a companion plant, but here I will focus on just five of the most commonly used.

Broadleaf Plantain (Plantago major)
Plantain is a common weed found across Europe and in North America. It was used for its medicinal properties, perhaps best known as the Soldier's Herb as it was used to dress wounds.

Plantain accumulates several micronutrients including magnesium, iron, manganese, calcium, sulfur, and iron, all of which will benefit your vegetables.

Allow plantain to die back naturally or dig it into the soil. You can cut the leaves monthly if you prefer and use them as a mulch. The plantain will, in most cases, grow back, but at the end of the season dig in the roots and leaves for maximum benefit.

Chickweed (Stellaria media)

This grows almost everywhere, but usually, it is an indication of soil with poor fertility. It accumulates potassium and phosphorus and will attract pollinators throughout its flowering season from spring to early summer. Chickweed is an edible plant, being treated like lettuce, and also has medicinal properties.

Leave chickweed to die back on its own for the best results, or cut the leaves regularly for mulch. Cutting the leaves and flowers will mean it doesn't attract as many pollinators. Dig this into the ground at the end of the season, so nutrients are reabsorbed back into the soil.

Lamb's Quarters (Chenopodium album)
This is common in poor soil and is used to improve the quality of it. The deep roots of lamb's quarters accumulate many vital nutrients including calcium, manganese, potassium, nitrogen, and phosphorus. The roots also loosen up the soil, helping to break up tough soil.

Treat this weed like the previous two to benefit your soil.

White Clover (Trifolium repens)

Commonly used as a green manure, but also found virtually everywhere as a wild herb, it grows happily in almost any soil, though loves clay. Digging clover into a clay soil will help condition the soil and improve it. It is also commonly found in soil that is low in nitrogen.

Clover fixes nitrogen into the soil as well as accumulating phosphorus. It attracts a wide variety of predatory insects including ladybugs and minute pirate bugs. As well as this, it attracts plenty of pollinating insects and provides shelter for spiders, ground beetles, parasitoid wasps and lacewings will lay they eggs on white clover. All in all, it is a very useful plant, even though it is a weed.

Use white clover in the same way as the previous weeds. It will grow rampantly so there are plenty of options for transplanting or gathering seeds to propagate it. Just make sure you keep it under control as it will take over if left to run wild.

Dandelion (Taraxacum officinale)
This is one of the most common weeds in most of our gardens and considered a real pest. Yet you can make wine out of the flowers, eat the leaves, and make coffee and beer from the roots. It is commonly found in hard clay soils, which it will loosen up as it grows.

Dandelions accumulate a variety of minerals including calcium, copper, iron, magnesium, silicon, potassium, and phosphorus. The flowers attract pollinators and ladybugs. It will also attract lacewings and parasitoid wasps, making it an ideal plant to have in your garden. Just make sure you remove and dispose of the spent flower so it can't spread seeds all over your garden!

Once they have finished flowering, dig up the dandelions and remove the roots, being careful not to leave any pieces or roots in the soil or attached to the leaves. Compost the leaves or dig them into the soil and destroy the roots. Dandelions grow back from even the tiniest piece of root and while they do benefit your soil, they can very easily take over your entire garden if left unchecked.

Weeds are a fantastic way of naturally improving your soil. Weeds tend to accumulate the minerals the soil needs and those with longer roots will help to loosen up hard soil. Although some weeds like poison ivy are annoying, others like stinging nettles are beneficial. If you want to keep the plants under control, then remove the seed heads before they can spread.

Endnote

Companion planting is something that not everyone will be familiar with or have heard of. It is a traditional method of gardening that has been developed through hundreds of generations of trial and error, passed on by word of mouth.

The basic principle is growing two plants next to each other that complement each other. This could mean that one keeps pests away from another or one conditions the soil for the other or one attracts pollinating insects, to mention just a few of the benefits. Many of us grow cucumbers and tomatoes next to each other in a greenhouse, often wondering why the cucumbers struggle. Yet when the cucumbers are moved away from the tomatoes, even to the other side of it, they will perk up and become healthier.

As more and more of us choose to follow a mostly organic approach to gardening, companion planting allows you to reduce your reliance on chemical sprays by using natural methods of pest control. By attracting the right types of insects into your garden, not just in their adult form but also as larvae, you will be able to keep pests to an acceptable level.

What most people don't realize is that chemical sprays kill indiscriminately. A chemical spray doesn't care if an insect is beneficial or harmful, it will kill them anyway. The real problem starts after use because many of these chemicals leave residues that the destructive insects don't mind, but the beneficial insects object to. A single chemical spray application could be enough to deter beneficial insects for the rest of the growing season, leaving your plot vulnerable to pests.

Obviously, you can see why this is considered a problem. There are a lot of other potential issues with chemical sprays which we won't go into here, but, needless to say, an organic approach to gardening is considered the best for you and the environment.

Companion planting can be different depending on where you are located. It is very much a trial and error method as you need to learn what works and doesn't work in your particular micro-environment. Most of the plants will work regardless of where you are located, but you need to be aware that some of these companion plants will not grow in all areas.

The best approach in these cases is to either use an alternative or to grow your companion plants in containers, bringing them inside over winter. Of course, for the more invasive companion plants such as mint and lemon balm, these are best grown in containers anyway otherwise they will take over your garden.

Combine companion planting with crop rotation, and you will be able to reduce the number of pests naturally. Remember that when rotating your crops this doesn't mean you need to rotate crops that are interplanted, e.g. Garlic plants dotted around your garden as companion plants. It's really about using your common sense here. If you discover a problem that attacks garlic in your garden, then stop growing it for a year or two until the problem goes away.

If you have suffered from your precious vegetable plants being destroyed by pests, then you will understand why companion planting is so very important. There is nothing more devastating than to go into your vegetable garden to find you crops have been decimated by pests that could have been prevented. In many cases, by the time you notice them, you are too late for companion planting, and chemical sprays will need to be used in large quantities. When it comes to treating pests in your vegetable garden, prevention really is better than a cure.

I like to grow brassicas, but several years ago my entire crop (over sixty plants) were destroyed by pests after I didn't manage to get into my vegetable garden for a couple of weeks. After that, I took a belt and braces approach to protecting my plants. My brassicas are planted in a specially prepared bed that is then netted to prevent pigeons (hugely destructive creatures) and cabbage white butterflies from getting to them. That is the first step in protecting them.

To take it a step further, onions and leeks are planted on either side of the brassicas in rows to provide extra protection. I grow mint in pots, and several of these pots are scattered around the brassica bed to deter flea beetles. I also grow rosemary in pots, and this too is left around the brassica bed to deter both cabbage flies and cabbage moths.

It may sound to you like overkill, but frankly, I am fed up of losing my hard work to pests. This companion planting ensures I get a fantastic crop every year and it also means I can get away with being slightly less vigilant at my vegetable plot. I know I cannot visit it every day, so companion planting gives me that extra level of protection and a bit more leeway.

Basil is well suited for growing with tomatoes and in my greenhouse, I will grow basil in pots interspersed with my tomato plants. Naturally, this improves the flavor of the tomatoes, but it also works well when I serve up the tomatoes in the kitchen.

Companion planting is an excellent way for you to protect your plants from pests naturally and organically, encouraging better growth. It is something anyone can practice, and most people grow many of these companion plants anyway, just not in the right locations. By switching around the location of some of your plants, you could very easily benefit from companion planting.

Start using companion planting in your garden and notice the difference in your plants and their health. It is surprising how effective this is, and it would be very easy for you to start locating plants together that benefit each other. Experiment with companion planting, and you can start seeing the benefits from it. The beneficial insects and pollinators it will attract are going to make a big difference to the quality and quantity of produce you get from your garden.

About Jason

Jason has been a keen gardener for over twenty years, having taken on numerous weed infested patches and turned them into productive vegetable gardens.

One of his first gardening experiences was digging over a 400 square foot garden in its entirety and turning it into a vegetable garden, much to the delight of his neighbors who all got free vegetables! It was through this experience that he discovered his love of gardening and started to learn more and more about the subject.

His first encounter with a greenhouse resulted in a tomato infested greenhouse but he soon learnt how to make the most of a greenhouse and now grows a wide variety of plants from grapes to squashes to tomatoes and more. Of course, his wife is delighted with his greenhouse as it means the windowsills in the house are no longer filled with seed trays every spring.

He is passionate about helping people learn to grow their own fresh produce and enjoy the many benefits that come with it, from the exercise of gardening to the nutrition of freshly picked produce. He often says that when you've tasted a freshly picked tomato you'll never want to buy another one from a store again!

Jason is also very active in the personal development community, having written books on self-help, including subjects such as motivation and confidence. He has also recorded over 80 hypnosis programs, being a fully qualified clinical hypnotist which he sells from his website www.MusicForChange.com.

He hopes that this book has been a pleasure for you to read and that you have learned a lot about the subject and welcomes your feedback either directly or through an Amazon review. This feedback is used to improve his books and provide better quality information for his readers.

Jason also loves to grow giant and unusual vegetables and is still planning on breaking the 400lb barrier with a giant pumpkin. He hopes that with his new allotment plot he'll be able to grow even more exciting vegetables to share with his readers.

Other Books By Jason

Please check out my other gardening books on Amazon, available in Kindle and paperback.

Berry Gardening – The Complete Guide to Berry Gardening from Gooseberries to Boysenberries and More
Who doesn't love fresh berries? Find out how you can grow many of the popular berries at home such as marionberries and blackberries and some of the more unusual like honeyberries and goji berries. A step by step guide to growing your own berries including pruning, propagating and more. Discover how you can grow a wide variety of berries at home in your garden or on your balcony.

Canning and Preserving at Home – A Complete Guide to Canning, Preserving and Storing Your Produce
A complete guide to storing your home-grown fruits and vegetables. Learn everything from how to freeze your produce to canning, making jams, jellies, and chutneys to dehydrating and more. Everything you need to know about storing your fresh produce, including some unusual methods of storage, some of which will encourage children to eat fresh fruit!

Container Gardening - Growing Vegetables, Herbs & Flowers in Containers
A step by step guide showing you how to create your very own container garden. Whether you have no garden, little space or you want to grow specific plants, this book guides you through everything you need to know about planting a container garden from the different types of pots, to which plants thrive in containers to handy tips helping you avoid the common mistakes people make with containers.

Cooking with Zucchini - Delicious Recipes, Preserves and More With Courgettes: How To Deal With A Glut Of Zucchini And Love It!

Getting too many zucchinis from your plants? This book teaches you how to grow your own courgettes at home as well as showing you the many different varieties you could grow. Packed full of delicious recipes, you will learn everything from the famous zucchini chocolate cake to delicious main courses, snacks, and Paleo diet friendly raw recipes. The must have guide for anyone dealing with a glut of zucchini.

Environmentally Friendly Gardening – Your Guide to a Sustainable, Eco-Friendly Garden

With a looming environmental crisis, we are all looking to do our bit to save the environment. This book talks you through how to garden in harmony with nature and reduce your environmental impact. Learn how to eliminate the need for chemicals with clever techniques and eco-friendly alternatives. Discover today how you can become a more environmentally friendly gardener and still have a beautiful garden.

Greenhouse Gardening - A Beginners Guide to Growing Fruit and Vegetables All Year Round

A complete, step by step guide to owning your own greenhouse. Learn everything you need to know from sourcing greenhouses to building foundations to ensuring it survives high winds. This handy guide will teach you everything you need to know to grow a wide range of plants in your greenhouse, including tomatoes, chilies, squashes, zucchini and much more. Find out how you can benefit from a greenhouse today, they are more fun and less work than you might think!

Growing Brassicas – Growing Cruciferous Vegetables from Broccoli to Mooli to Wasabi and More

Brassicas are renowned for their health benefits and are packed full of vitamins. They are easy to grow at home but beset by problems. Find out how you can grow these amazing vegetables at home, including the incredibly beneficial plants broccoli and maca. Includes step by step growing guides plus delicious recipes for every recipe!

Growing Chilies – A Beginners Guide to Growing, Using & Surviving Chilies

Ever wanted to grow super-hot chilies? Or maybe you just want to grow your own chilies to add some flavor to your food? This book is your complete, step-by-step guide to growing chilies at home. With topics from selecting varieties to how to germinate seeds, you will learn everything you need to know to grow chilies successfully, even the notoriously difficult to grow varieties such as Carolina Reaper. With recipes for sauces, meals and making your own chili powder, you'll find everything you need to know to grow your own chili plants

Growing Fruit: The Complete Guide to Growing Fruit at Home

This is a complete guide to growing fruit from apricots to walnuts and everything in between. You will learn how to choose fruit plants, how to grow and care for them, how to store and preserve the fruit and much more. With recipes, advice, and tips this is the perfect book for anyone who wants to learn more about growing fruit at home, whether beginner or experienced gardener.

Growing Garlic – A Complete Guide to Growing, Harvesting & Using Garlic

Everything you need to know to grow this popular plant. Whether you are growing normal garlic or elephant garlic for cooking or health, you will find this book contains all the information you need. Traditionally a difficult crop to grow with a long growing season, you'll learn the exact conditions garlic needs, how to avoid the common problems people encounter and how to store your garlic for use all year round. A complete, step-by-step guide showing you precisely how to grow garlic at home.

Growing Herbs – A Beginners Guide to Growing, Using, Harvesting and Storing Herbs

A comprehensive guide to growing herbs at home, detailing 49 different herbs. Learn everything you need to know to grow these herbs from their preferred soil conditions to how to harvest and propagate them and more. Including recipes for health and beauty plus delicious dishes to make in your kitchen. This step-by-step guide is designed to teach you all about growing herbs at home, from a few herbs in containers to a fully-fledged herb garden. An indispensable guide to growing and using herbs.

Growing Giant Pumpkins – How to Grow Massive Pumpkins at Home

A complete step by step guide detailing everything you need to know to produce pumpkins weighing hundreds of pounds, if not edging into the thousands! Anyone can grow giant pumpkins at home, and this book gives you the insider secrets of the giant pumpkin growers showing you how to avoid the mistakes people commonly make when trying to grow a giant pumpkin. This is a complete guide detailing everything from preparing the soil to getting the right seeds to germinating the seeds and caring for your pumpkins.

Growing Lavender: Growing, Using, Cooking and Healing with Lavender

A complete guide to growing and using this beautiful plant. Find out about the hundreds of different varieties of lavender and how you can grow this bee friendly plant at home. With hundreds of uses in crafts, cooking and healing, this plant has a long history of association with humans. Discover today how you can grow lavender at home and enjoy this amazing herb.

Growing Tomatoes: Your Guide to Growing Delicious Tomatoes at Home

This is the definitive guide to growing delicious and fresh tomatoes at home. Teaching you everything from selecting seeds to planting and caring for your tomatoes as well as diagnosing problems this is the ideal book for anyone who wants to grow tomatoes at home. A comprehensive must have guide.

How to Compost – Turn Your Waste into Brown Gold

This is a complete step by step guide to making your own compost at home. Vital to any gardener, this book will explain everything from setting up your compost heap to how to ensure you get fresh compost in just a few weeks. A must have handbook for any gardener who wants their plants to benefit from home-made compost.

How to Grow Potatoes - The Guide to Choosing, Planting and Growing in Containers Or the Ground

Learn everything you need to know about growing potatoes at home. Discover the wide variety of potatoes you can grow, many delicious varieties you will never see in the shops. Find out the best way to grow potatoes at home, how to protect your plants from the many pests and diseases and how to store your harvest so you can enjoy fresh potatoes over winter. A complete step by step guide telling you everything you need to know to grow potatoes at home successfully.

Hydroponics: A Beginners Guide to Growing Food without Soil

Hydroponics is growing plants without soil, which is a fantastic idea for indoor gardens. It is surprisingly easy to set up, once you know what you are doing and is significantly more productive and quicker than growing in soil. This book will tell you everything you need to know to get started growing flowers, vegetables, and fruit hydroponically at home.

Indoor Gardening for Beginners: The Complete Guide to Growing Herbs, Flowers, Vegetables and Fruits in Your House

Discover how you can grow a wide variety of plants in your home. Whether you want to grow herbs for cooking, vegetables or a decorative plant display, this book tells you everything you need to know. Learn which plants to keep in your home to purify the air and remove harmful chemicals and how to successfully grow plants from cacti to flowers to carnivorous plants.

Keeping Chickens for Beginners – Keeping Backyard Chickens from Coops to Feeding to Care and More

Chickens are becoming very popular to keep at home, but it isn't something you should leap into without the right information. This book guides you through everything you need to know to keep chickens from decided what breed to what coop to how to feed them, look after them and keep your chickens healthy and producing eggs. This is your complete guide to owning chickens, with absolutely everything you need to know to get started and successfully keep chickens at home.

Raised Bed Gardening – A Guide to Growing Vegetables In Raised Beds

Learn why raised beds are such an efficient and effortless way to garden as you discover the benefits of no-dig gardening, denser planting and less bending, ideal for anyone who hates weeding or suffers from back pain. You will learn everything you need to know to build your own raised beds, plant them and ensure they are highly productive.

Save Our Bees – Your Guide to Creating a Bee Friendly Environment

Discover the plight of our bees and why they desperately need all of our help. Find out all about the different bees, how they are harmless, yet a vital part of our food chain. This book teaches you all about bees and how you can create a bee friendly environment in your neighborhood. You will learn the plants bees love, where they need to live and what plants are dangerous for bees, plus lots, lots more.

Vertical Gardening: Maximum Productivity, Minimum Space

This is an exciting form of gardening allows you to grow large amounts of fruit and vegetables in small areas, maximizing your use of space. Whether you have a large garden, an allotment or just a small balcony, you will be able to grow more delicious fresh produce. Find out how I grew over 70 strawberry plants in just three feet of ground space and more in this detailed guide.

Worm Farming: Creating Compost at Home with Vermiculture
Learn about this amazing way of producing high-quality compost at home by recycling your kitchen waste. Worms break it down and produce a sought after, highly nutritious compost that your plants will thrive in. No matter how big your garden you will be able to create your own worm farm and compost using the techniques in this step-by-step guide. Learn how to start worm farming and producing your own high-quality compost at home.

Want More Inspiring Gardening Ideas?

This book is part of the Inspiring Gardening Ideas series. Bringing you the best books anywhere on how to get the most from your garden or allotment. Please remember to leave a review on Amazon once you have finished this book as it helps me continually improve my books.

You can find out about more wonderful books just like this one at: www.GardeningWithJason.com

Follow me at www.YouTube.com/OwningAnAllotment for my video diary and tips. Join me on Facebook for regular updates and discussions at www.Facebook.com/OwningAnAllotment.

Find me on Instagram and Twitter as @allotmentowner where I post regular updates, offers and gardening news. Follow me today and let's catch up in person!

Free Book!

Visit http://gardeningwithjason.com/your-free-book/ now for your free copy of my book "Environmentally Friendly Gardening" sent to your inbox. Discover today how you can become a more eco-friendly gardener and help us all make the world a better place.

This book is full of tips and advice, helping you to reduce your need for chemicals and work in harmony with nature to improve the environment. With the looming crisis, there is something we can all do in our gardens, no matter how big or small they are and they can still look fantastic!

Thank you for reading!

Printed in Great Britain
by Amazon